The Importance of Jesus Being God

Daniel S. Smith

Kingdom Publishers

Copyright© Daniel S. Smith 2025

All rights reserved. No part of this book may be reproduced in any form by photocopying or any electronic or mechanical means, including information storage or retrieval systems, without permission in writing from both the copyright owner and the publisher of the book. The right of Daniel S. Smith to be identified as the author of this work has been asserted by him in accordance with the Copyright, Designs, and Patents Act 1988 and any subsequent amendments thereto.

A catalogue record for this book is available from the British Library.

All Scripture quotations have been taken from The New International version of the Bible

ISBN: 978-1-916801-46-2

1st Edition 2025 by Kingdom Publishers, London, UK.

You can purchase copies of this book from any leading bookstore or at: **www.kingdompublishers.co.uk**

Contents

Introduction	1
Chapter 1. How the New Testament declares the Deity of Jesus	**3**
a) Direct proclamation	4
b) The transference of Old Testament language about God	7
c) Jesus fulfils Old Testament prophecies and expectations	10
Chapter 2. God makes Himself known	**14**
a) Through creation	14
b) Through ancient Israel	15
c) Through Jesus Christ	18
Chapter 3. Jesus, the only Saviour	**23**
a) Salvation in Jesus alone	23
b) Redemption and rescue	24
c) Forgiveness of sins	28
d) Reconciliation and relationship with God	30
e) Holiness and eternal life	32
Chapter 4. Jesus, the suffering God	**35**
a) Jesus suffered for us	35
b) God and the problem of suffering	38

Chapter 5. Jesus, the eternal and supreme Lord   **47**

    a) King of kings and Lord of lords   47

    b) Jesus is to be worshipped   52

    c) Jesus is to be proclaimed   55

    d) Jesus is to be followed   57

Chapter 6. Jesus and the 'I am' sayings   **60**

    a) I am the Bread of Life   61

    b) I am the Light of the World   62

    c) I am the Gate   63

    d) I am the Good Shepherd   64

    e) I am the Resurrection and the Life   66

    f) I am the Way, the Truth, and the Life   67

    g) I am the True Vine   68

Chapter 7. Jesus is 'God with us'   **71**

    a) God's desire to be with us   72

    b) The dilemma of separation   72

    c) God's plan to dwell with His people   73

    d) Jesus came to us as 'God with us'   74

    e) Salvation as 'God with us'   76

    f) God's eternal dwelling with His people   78

Conclusion   **80**

Bibliography   **82**

Introduction

I grew up with something of a Christian background. My dad was converted when I was 5, and so I ended up going to Sunday school for a few years, until around the age of 10 or 11. When I got older, I wasn't interested in going to church anymore. I still believed there was a God and about Jesus, but it didn't mean anything to me, and it didn't impact my life.

When, however, I was 22, I started to be compelled to go to church again, largely, I think, because my brother, out of the blue, became a Christian. When I did, I started to be interested, and eventually I accepted Jesus and received the peace of the Holy Spirit. I came to know the living God personally. This filled a deep sense of something missing in my life, which had troubled me for many years as a teenager, but never since.

That is just a brief testimony of my personal story, which is one of billions who have encountered Jesus in a very real and personal way. I will share some other experiences of Jesus throughout this book, but the focus will be on seeing what the Bible says, since it is from that source we can identify the reality of Jesus ourselves, if we genuinely seek Him.

The importance of Jesus Christ is clearly evident and unmistakable in world history. Over 2000 years, He has become possibly the most talked about figure in history, having more followers than anyone else, spanning across time, nations and cultures. There are followers of Jesus in more or less every part of the world today. Some of these followers, including most of His first disciples, were willing to die for their faith in Jesus and that He had been raised from the dead. The New Testament records the first martyr, Stephen, one who not only witnessed to his experience of

Jesus but died for it (Acts 7:54-60), as well as several others in the mid-first century. A martyr is simply a witness. It became attached to those who died for their beliefs through persecution.

Then there is the apostle Paul, who gave his approval of the death of Stephen, followed by a campaign of persecution against the Lord's people. *"He went to the high priest and asked him for letters to the synagogues in Damascus, so that if he found any there who belonged to the Way, whether men or women, he might take them as prisoners to Jerusalem"* (Acts 9:1-2). Yet he was halted in his tracks when he encountered the risen Jesus. From that time on, he was completely changed and became the most famous missionary in Christian history, as well as writing nearly one-third of the New Testament.

These examples illustrate that this Jesus is hugely significant and life-changing for many who encounter Him. He cannot be just an amazing teacher or inspirational leader. This book will seek to show not only that Jesus is divine, but what difference that can make, not just in our theology, but in our experience of Jesus in our lives, and the implications for the wider world.

The words 'deity'/'divine' in this book refer to the Christian understanding of God as Father, Son and Holy Spirit, the Holy Trinity, 3 'persons' but 1 God. The term 'Trinity' does not appear in the Bible but was coined by Tertullian in the third century to describe their understanding of God as '3-persons-in-1-being'. Tertullian based his understanding on the New Testament teaching about God. It is difficult to describe the concept of the Trinity in our limited language and minds. We should expect God to be greater than our comprehension. This does not need to be a barrier to us coming to know God and experience Him in our lives.

To begin with, we shall see how the New Testament declares the Deity of Jesus. This is a little technical, so some may find it helpful to start at Chapter 2.

Chapter 1. How the New Testament declares the Deity of Jesus

The name Jesus occurs in all 27 New Testament books with over 1300 occurrences, except for the short letter of 3 John. This alone shows how Jesus is of central importance to the New Testament, and thus our understanding of God and the Bible as a whole. The name Jesus does not occur in the Old Testament, as it refers to the creation account and the history of Israel prior to the time of Jesus being born in Bethlehem. Jesus is part of the divine Godhead and existed before His miraculous incarnation when He became human, born of the virgin Mary. He received the name 'Jesus' at His birth as directed by an angel of the Lord to Joseph in a dream, *"...you are to give him the name Jesus, because he will save his people from their sins"* (Matthew 1:21). The name derives from Hebrew words for 'saving', or 'saviour,' and was probably pronounced 'Yeshua.' It has had various linguistic changes according to many languages used in translations: 'Isa', 'Yesu', 'Jesu', etc.

So, how does the New Testament declare the deity of Jesus? There are essentially three ways that show this:

a) Direct proclamation of Jesus as God

b) Transference of Old Testament language about God to Jesus

c) Jesus fulfils Old Testament prophecies which relate to God's anticipated salvation and action in the world for His people

Let's take each of these in turn.

a) Direct proclamation

The use of the word 'God' in the Bible nearly always refers to the one true and eternal God who created the universe, revealing Himself to Abraham, Moses, the nation of Israel and the prophets in the Old Testament. In the New Testament period, we see an understanding of God as Father, Son, and Holy Spirit, often referred to as the 'Trinity' in much of church history. The understanding of God, as '3-in-1' is also present in the Old Testament, but brought to light more clearly in Jesus and the New Testament.

In the New Testament, the word 'God' is used numerous times with reference to the Father specifically, with Jesus being referred to most frequently by His name, but also titles such as Lord, Christ / Messiah, Son of God, or Son of Man, as Jesus often used of Himself. This distinction is common and often helps us to see how the New Testament writers understood and experienced the different members of the Trinity in their different roles. There are a few times, though, where Jesus is directly referred to as God. Let's take the opening of John's gospel:

"In the beginning was the Word, and the Word was with God, and the Word was God." (John 1:1)

"The Word became flesh and made his dwelling among us. We have seen his glory, the glory of the one and only Son, who came from the Father, full of grace and truth." (John 1:14)

John has some of the clearest references to the deity of Jesus in the New Testament. In its opening 18 verses, Jesus is referred to several times as *'the Word'*. The first verse shows Jesus was not only *'with God'* at the beginning of creation, but He also *'was God'*. This shows something of the complex nature of God, who far exceeds our limited human comprehension, as remarkable as our brains are.

We are not attempting to understand the Trinity here but rather understand how the Bible shows Jesus is God, and then, what that means for us. The main point from these opening verses for us here is that Jesus, *'the Word'*, is eternal and is God. As the opening statement at the very opening of John's gospel, it highlights the central importance of the identity of Jesus for John's gospel. Ben Witherington suggests the whole of John's gospel is to be read in light of this first verse; the deeds and words of a divine, eternal being.[1]

Jesus, *'the Word'*, is not distant and unknowable; He became human and lived among us. The term 'Word' implies communication of the revelation of, in this case, God. We will discuss the significance of this verse more below. Here, I will just point out that this shows that Jesus is both God and human, and so is able to relate closely to us and our experiences in life (cf. Hebrews 4:14-16). Jesus reveals God to us (Chapter 2) and is God with us (Chapter 7).

Near the end of John's gospel, after Jesus rose from the dead following His crucifixion, He appeared to His disciples on several occasions. When Jesus appeared to Thomas, we read His response from Thomas in realising not just that Jesus was miraculously alive, but his understanding of what this meant about who Jesus is. *"Thomas said to him, 'My Lord and my God!"* (John 20:28). This statement is directed at Jesus, who then affirms that what Thomas has said is a true declaration of belief. *"Because you have seen me, you have believed...that I am alive."* (John 20:29). The resurrection of Jesus authenticates His lordship and deity.

In the New Testament letters, we also see Jesus directly called 'God'. We read the following in Titus 2:11-14:

---

[1] Ben Witherington, *John's Wisdom: A Commentary on the Fourth Gospel*, (Louisville, MN: Westminster John Knox Press, 1995), p. 54.

> *"For the grace of God has appeared that offers salvation to all people. It teaches us to say 'No' to ungodliness and worldly passions, and to live self-controlled, upright and godly lives in this present age, while we wait for the blessed hope – the appearing of the glory of our great God and Saviour, Jesus Christ, who gave himself for us to redeem us from all wickedness and to purify for himself a people that are his very own, eager to do what is good."*

The apostle Paul here refers to the appearing of the glory of the Lord in His Second Coming. In so doing, he calls Jesus *'our great God and Saviour'*. In the Greek text, 'God' and 'Saviour' are both governed by the article (the), and are both in the genitive case, as also is 'Jesus Christ'. This simply means that Paul is not referring to 'our God' and 'our Saviour Jesus Christ' separately, but as one and the same. This is confirmed in that Paul uses the phrase *'God our Saviour'* in Titus 1:3 and 3:4 in reference to God the Father. It is also a common understanding in the New Testament that Jesus is coming again, and His appearing, or revealing, is referred to on numerous occasions by different New Testament writers, and by Jesus Himself (e.g., Mark 14:62; 1 Timothy 6:14; 2 Peter 1:16; 1 John 3:2).

One other explicit reference occurs in Hebrews 1:8-9, where we read these words:

> *"But about the Son he says, 'Your throne, O God, will last forever and ever; a sceptre of justice will be the sceptre of your kingdom. You have loved righteousness and hated wickedness; therefore God, your God, has set you above your companions by anointing you with the oil of joy."*

The writer to the Hebrews is describing how Jesus, the Son of God, is greater than the angels. In these verses, the Son is directly called God, quoting Psalm 45:6-7 from the Old Testament. In this Psalm, it is the human king of Israel who is addressed as 'God' as the representative on earth. This foreshadows Jesus, who is the true king of God's kingdom, but more than just His representative: Jesus is the exact representation of God's being and is greater than even the angels who are called to worship Him (Hebrews 1:3, 6).

Again, we see a clear reference to the deity of Jesus, and as in John 1:1, also a reference to God as distinct *'your God'* yet still the same God. We may also note here that while John 1:1 does not contain the article (the) in Greek, leading some to see falsely that it means 'a god'; however, the article is present when it is used here in Hebrews 1:8. The lack of the article in John 1:1 is a matter of Greek syntax.[2]

So, we see several clear references to Jesus as God, which are perhaps the most affirmative and obvious declarations of His deity. This leads to the way in which the New Testament most often declares the deity of Jesus, which is not so obvious to those unfamiliar with the Old Testament, in using Old Testament language about God to talk about Jesus and what He did.

b) The transference of Old Testament language about God

There are many references to the Old Testament in the New. Many of these are about Jesus in some manner, and some are direct parallels with God in the Old Testament. Probably the most famous of these are the 'I am' sayings in John's gospel. This is most important as it refers to God's name declared to Moses in Exodus 3:14, *"I am who I am"*. The same words in the Greek version of the Old Testament (*ego eimi – I am*) are then used by Jesus to describe who He is in John's 'I am' sayings. At least two of these: *"I am the light of the world"* (John 8:12), and *"I am the good shepherd"* (John 10:11, 14), are also descriptions of God in the Old Testament: *"The*

---

[2] See Andreas J. Köstenberger, Benjamin L. Merkle, and Robert L. Plummer, *Going Deeper with New Testament Greek*, (Nashville, TN: B&H Academic, 2016), p. 50.

Lord is my light" in Psalm 27:1, and *"The Lord is my Shepherd"* from Psalm 23:1. Jesus also declared in John 8:58, *"Before Abraham was, I am"*, to which the religious leaders were ready to stone Him for blasphemy. They understood He was invoking the divine Name for Himself. We will see more of the significance of these statements in Chapter 6.

In the Gospels, Jesus also does things that only God can do. In Matthew 8, Mark 4 and Luke 8, we see the account of Jesus calming the storm. His disciples were amazed and terrified at such a miracle, having control over nature (Luke 8:25). No ordinary person can do such a thing. In Psalm 107:29, we see it is the Lord who indeed can still the storms, *"He stilled the storm to a whisper; the waves of the sea were hushed."*

In Mark 2 and Luke 5, Jesus heals a paralysed man, but He also proclaims forgiveness for the man's sins. The religious leaders believed He was blaspheming because only God can forgive sins (Mark 2:7; Luke 5:21). Jesus proved He can forgive sins by healing the man. By so doing, Jesus showed He is more than a prophet and has divine authority. Jesus performed many miracles, as did some of the Old Testament prophets, because the Holy Spirit was upon Him (Luke 4:18). Yet Jesus was unique in His closeness to God the Father and only did what He saw His Father doing.

> *"Jesus gave them this answer: 'Very truly I tell you, the Son can do nothing by himself; he can do only what he sees his Father doing, because whatever the Father does the Son also does. For the Father loves the Son and shows him all he does. Yes, and he will show him even greater works than these, so that you will be amazed. For just as the Father raises the dead and gives them life, even so the Son gives life to whom he is pleased to give it. Moreover, the Father judges no one, but has entrusted all judgement to the Son, that all may honour the Son just as they*

honour the Father. Whoever does not honour the Son does not honour the Father, who sent him." (John 5:19-23)

Not only does Jesus declare He is doing the works of His Father, He also declares He has received authority to give life and to judge, and so receive the same honour that is due God the Father. This goes beyond any privilege of Old Testament prophets. Wright similarly states that, *'Jesus does what only God can do... The Old Testament affirms that [God] alone is the universal creator, ruler, judge and Saviour. According to the New Testament, Jesus performs those exact same roles and functions.'*[3]

Let us now turn to the epistles, the letters written to the early churches by the apostles, those sent out by Jesus (Acts 1:8).

We see in the letters of Paul some profound statements about Jesus that are used exclusively of God in the Old Testament. In Philippians 2:10-11, we read.

"Therefore, God exalted him to the highest place and gave him the name that is above every name, that at the name of Jesus every knee should bow, in heaven and on earth and under the earth, and every tongue acknowledge that Jesus Christ is Lord, to the glory of God the Father."

This, in itself, is a profound statement: because Jesus humbled Himself so completely, not using His equality with God to His own advantage (2:6). He became a human, a slave, and gave Himself over to death on a cross (2:7-9). He has now received the name above all names, to whom every person and every creature will bow, to the Father's glory. Verse 11 is a direct reference to God in the Old Testament as declared through Isaiah.

---

[3] Christopher. J. H. Wright, *Knowing God Through The Old Testament*, (Downers Grove, IL: IVP, 2019), p. 225.

"By myself I have sworn, my mouth has uttered in all integrity a word that will not be revoked: before me every knee will bow; by me every tongue will swear." (Isaiah 45:23)

This reference, which Paul would have had in mind, being steeped in the Old Testament, is meant to leave no question in doubt that Jesus has equality with God and is worthy of the same honour and worship as the Father. It is no coincidence that the language in these two texts resonates. Paul transfers this assertion of the One God of Israel and uses it to show Jesus' equality with the God of Israel. Philippians 2:6 also shows that Jesus existed before He was born a human, alluding to His eternal nature.

The eternal nature of Jesus which gives Him that equality with God is also described in the last New Testament book, in two connected statements that bookend Revelation: *"I am the Alpha and the Omega,' says the Lord God, 'who is, and who was, and who is to come, the Almighty'* (1:8). Then later Jesus says, *'I am the Alpha and the Omega, the First and the Last, the Beginning and the End"* (22:13). The eternal nature of God is clearly evidenced throughout the Old Testament (e.g., Genesis 21:33; Psalm 111:10; Isaiah 26:4) upon which Revelation is heavily based for much of its language and themes. Jesus is described with that same language here.

These are just a selection of texts which show how 'God-language' from the Old Testament is transferred to Jesus in the New Testament. This is the main way the New Testament declares Jesus' deity. We shall consider one other, in how Jesus fulfils Old Testament Scripture.

c) Jesus fulfils Old Testament prophecies and expectations

Around 600 years before Jesus, the nation of Israel, as God's people, was taken into exile by Babylon in three waves. After Babylon fell to Persia, Cyrus allowed the Jews to return to

Jerusalem in 536 BC. During this Jewish exile, several prophets began to speak of a new act of God for His people. Part of this was in God promising the Jews He would return them home. Even after this, however, many concluded that the exile was not truly over, as they had no official king, and God's glory did not return to the new temple (Ezra 3:10-13). There became an expectation for God to come to His people for their salvation from the words God spoke to Israel's prophets. I note just two here which have particular relevance to the deity of Jesus.

First, we read in Malachi 3:1, likely the last Old Testament prophet around 400 BC:

"I will send my messenger, who will prepare the way before me. Then suddenly the Lord you are seeking will come to his temple; the messenger of the covenant, whom you desire, will come,' says the LORD Almighty."

In this passage, the LORD says He is going to send a messenger to prepare the way before Him. Along with many other prophecies, this led to an expectation among the Jewish people that He was going to raise up a messianic figure to truly restore the nation of Israel. By the time of Jesus, this expectation was essentially that God would establish a new king and deliver Israel from Roman rule. The messenger in which Malachi spoke of (also Isaiah 40:3-5), is declared in the New Testament to be John the Baptist, who prepared the way for Jesus (Matthew 3:1-3; Mark 1:1-4; Luke 3:1-6; John 1:23). God Himself was going to come to His people, and would come to '*His*' temple; that can only be God. The New Testament shows us that Jesus is the promised One to come, although many did not recognise Him at the time (John 1:10-11). John also testifies that Jesus is the new Temple of God (2:21), and the glory of God (1:14), which did not return to the second temple after the exile, because in Jesus is the full presence of God, the gateway between heaven and earth (John 1:51).

Secondly, in the period of Israel's return from exile, Zechariah had several prophecies, including this remarkable declaration in Zechariah 12:10.

> *"And I will pour out on the house of David and the inhabitants of Jerusalem a Spirit of grace and supplication. They will look on me, the one they have pierced, and they will mourn for him as one mourns for an only child, and grieve bitterly for him as one grieves for a firstborn son."*

Again, the context is the LORD speaking. What is striking here is that there will be a time when the inhabitants of Jerusalem will look on (or 'to') me, the LORD, whom they pierced. If one asks when God was pierced, the only answer can be on the Cross, where Jesus died, on the hill of Golgotha outside Jerusalem. This is a prophecy looking forward to Jesus, just as He was going to die to fulfil other Old Testament prophecy, signalling the immense importance of His death as we shall see in Chapter 3. (see also, Isaiah 53; Psalm 22). The context of Zechariah 10 suggests a battle of some sort, in which, despite victory, there is also grief because of loss. Indeed, it is God's own people, the Israelites, who would have God's representative put to death. However, Jesus' death is prophesied as a victory, as Barry Webb notes. '*The victory that will usher in the kingdom of God will not be won without suffering, and none will suffer more keenly than [God] Himself*',[4] which we see in Jesus. Yet this did not spell the end of God's people, but rather opened the way to the outpouring of God's grace and forgiveness by His Spirit (see also Isaiah 32:15; Joel 2:28-32; Ezekiel 39:29).[5]

---

[4] Barry Webb: *The Message of Zechariah*, The Bible Speaks Today (IVP, Leicester, 2003), p. 160.

[5] Webb, *The Message of Zechariah*, p. 161.

It is basically impossible that, just by chance, Jesus could fulfil the vast number of Old Testament Scriptures, as declared in the New Testament. If one reads Isaiah 53, for example, it is striking how many details speak of what Jesus later did, and what He suffered 700 years later.

These examples of quotations, references and prophecies show clearly that Jesus indeed fulfils Scripture and at the same time show His deity from a New Testament perspective. This is more than just a theological or abstract idea, it gives us a solid basis to then discuss the implications of His deity. Why does it matter to us that Jesus is God? The identity of Jesus is of central importance in the New Testament's declaration of Jesus and His fulfilment of Old Testament Scripture. This question we will now explore in the following chapters.

Chapter 2. God makes Himself known

People will sometimes ask, 'If there is a God, why does He not just reveal Himself to the world?' This is a reasonable point, to which the biblical witness and Christian experience of faith can, in fact, answer. God has indeed made Himself known. There are essentially three ways that we see this.

a) Through creation

Firstly, God has revealed Himself through the natural order of creation, which the Bible clearly affirms was created solely by the one eternal God who is not created. The first verse of the Bible affirms this truth: *"In the beginning God created the heavens and the earth."* (Genesis 1:1)

Much could be said about the magnificence, complexity and beauty of the universe, even just the comparably tiny earth we live on, or the far smaller human body. The creation's order and majesty speak of the One who created it. Romans 1:20 tells us, *"For since the creation of the world God's invisible qualities – his eternal power and divine nature – have been clearly seen, being understood from what has been made, so that people are without excuse."* What we see in the world is a reflection of God's divine nature, His beauty, a sophisticated mind that displays His eternal power, bringing creation into existence with a simple word (Genesis 1:3). If the big bang theory is correct, perhaps that was the result of when God spoke the universe into existence out of nothing (Hebrews 11:3; cf. Genesis 1:1-26).

Yet what we see in the context of Romans 1 is that people have suppressed the truth about God because of wickedness (1:19). In so doing they became darkened in their thinking (1:21), exchanging the truth about God for a lie, worshipping and serving created things rather than the Creator (1:25). Our minds tend to doubt the very existence of our Creator because of sin. It was because of sin that humans were first banished from God's presence in the Garden of Eden (Genesis 3:22-24). This explains the 'absence of God' that people naturally feel and often question in their minds. But God is still revealed in creation to us if we are willing to accept it. Why else should we marvel at the beauty and magnificence of the world if it does not reveal something of the One who made it? Even so, this is only a partial revelation of God, of His existence and what He is like. God has revealed Himself to humanity in history in two further and greater ways.

b) Through ancient Israel

Secondly, God revealed Himself in history to ancient Israel as recorded in the Old Testament. This was over a period of hundreds of years, through appearing to different people at various times, and through speaking His word to the people through various prophets. God revealed Himself to Abraham, Isaac, Jacob, and to Moses and the Israelites when He delivered Israel out of slavery in Egypt. God spoke to Abraham at several points where He made promises to Abraham, His descendants, and promised to bless all nations through him. This was the beginning of God's plan to bring back humanity after going astray in the Garden of Eden.

> *"The LORD had said to Abram, 'Go from your country, your people and your father's household to the land I will show you. 'I will make you into a great nation, and I will bless you; I will make your name great, and you will be a blessing. I will bless those who bless you, and whoever curses you I will curse; and all peoples on earth will be blessed through you." (Genesis 12:3)*

This is a key text for what God would eventually do in forming the nation of Israel, giving them the land of Canaan, and bringing blessing to all nations through one of Abraham's descendants. God spoke to Abraham several other times (Genesis

15, 17, 18, 22), which were key points of God revealing His promises to Abraham. God is said to have revealed Himself to Jacob when he was fleeing from his brother (Genesis 35:7). This was the first time Jacob had encountered God. Again, it is associated with God's promises to Jacob and the fulfilment of His promises originally to Abraham (Genesis 28:13-15). Jacob even wrestled with God and saw Him face to face (Genesis 32:22-32), where Jacob had a real sense of his need for God's blessing. The encounter profoundly shaped and changed Jacob. So, we see here also the personal experience of God as a significant way in which God was starting to reveal Himself.

God's revelation to Moses was even more dramatic, in appearing to Moses in the burning bush, where God promised to free His people from slavery through Moses (Exodus 3). This was accompanied by many signs in the plagues against Egypt and the crossing of the Red Sea (Exodus 7-14). This was a dramatic revelation of God's mighty power to perform miracles to save His people. He subsequently revealed Himself in cloud and fire to Israel on Mount Sinai (Exodus 19:10-19). This was when God made a covenant – or a contractual promise – with Israel to be *"a kingdom of priests and a holy nation"* (19:6), and He would be their God; then He gave them the terms of the covenant of how they were to live as His people and worship Him alone (Exodus 20:1–23:19).

God had now fulfilled His promise to Abraham to make him and his offspring into a great nation and would continue to fulfil His other promises. Moses is also said to have spoken face to face with God as a friend (Exodus 33:11) to the point his face would radiate after being in God's presence (Exodus 34:30).

There is also a progression of knowledge of the LORD in Exodus, in His revealing who He is first to Moses, and then to both Israel and to Pharaoh in the plagues. For example, the plagues demonstrated there is no one like the LORD (8:10), He is God in Egypt (8:22), but also God over the whole earth (9:14). God would bring His people out of Egypt that He may be known by them, and they would be His people (6:7), be known by them as Provider (16:8), and the One who makes them holy (31:13). This culminates in God's revealing of His glory to Moses and proclamation of His divine character, which became the most quoted text in the Old Testament, a pivotal text in Israel's understanding of who God is.

> *"And he passed in front of Moses, proclaiming, 'The LORD, the LORD, the compassionate and gracious God, slow to anger, abounding in love and faithfulness, maintaining love to thousands, and forgiving wickedness, rebellion and sin. Yet he does not leave the guilty unpunished; he punishes the children and their children for the sin of the parents to the third and fourth generation." (34:6-7)*

We should note here that the revelation of God is centred on His character, His divine love and judgement upon evil. The emphasis in this passage is clearly on God's divine mercy and forgiveness rather than His anger (a thousand generations compared with three or four). At the same time, Israel should not assume God's forgiveness without noting the risk of punishment.[6] God's desire to forgive rather than condemn becomes very clear in the New Testament (e.g. 2 Peter 3:9).

The many narratives in the Old Testament show how people understood and experienced God's interaction, working, equipping, and guidance in everyday life and as God's people. The Psalms are a key place where we see people's experience of God rooted in the joys and struggles of everyday life. Over the course of Israel's

---

[6] Leander E. Keck, *The New Interpreter's Bible, vol. 1: Genesis, Exodus, Leviticus*, (Nashville, TN: Abingdon Press, 1994), p. 947,48.

history, they learned much about who God is, what He can do, and what it means to be His people.

c) Through Jesus Christ

The written word of God in both the Old and New Testaments reveals God much more clearly than the creation. This culminates in one more revelation, which is key to our knowledge of God, in the person of Jesus Christ. This is the full revelation of God, and the full knowledge of His salvation made known to all people in His Son. In the opening of the letter of Hebrews, we read:

> *"In the past God spoke to our ancestors through the prophets at many times and in various ways, but in these last days he has spoken to us by his Son, whom he appointed heir of all things, and through whom also he made the universe. The Son is the radiance of God's glory and the exact representation of his being, sustaining all things by his powerful word." (1:1-3a)*

We see here how God has spoken, made Himself known in a new way in His Son, through whom the universe was made, and who is the exact likeness of God. The Son radiates, reflects the glory of God. As sunlight makes known the sun in all its splendour, so Jesus makes known God in His eternal glory, because the Son is *'the exact representation of his being'*. It is in Jesus that we can now fully see God; what He is like, and who He is as Lord and Saviour. He is no longer hidden in a cloud, only revealing Himself closely to a few chosen individuals. The revelation and knowledge of God are now available to all who come to Jesus. When we see Jesus, the darkness of ignorance about God caused by sin is dispelled. The eyes of our heart our enlightened (Ephesians 1:18), both in our mental understanding about God, and in personal experience of the reality of God in our inner being. Through faith in Jesus, we can now know God personally through the gift of the Holy Spirit, whom He gives to all who believe (Acts 2:38).

For myself, I knew things *about* God while growing up, but it did not impact my life. When I came to know Jesus personally for myself, I received the gift of the Holy Spirit who gave me a peace and joy in God which I had not known before (Romans 14:17); He helped me to understand the spiritual reality of God's word and the gift of salvation in Jesus Christ (1 Corinthians 2:11-14), and began to work in me God's character, especially in the sense of love and taking away hate I had for certain people, without me even thinking much about it (Galatians 5:22-23). These experiences of knowing God are all affirmed by God's word. I tried to read the Bible at one point when I was a teenager, but only for a few days at the most. I had no desire to do so. When I became a Christian, I had a desire to read God's word without anyone telling me to do so.

God speaks by His written word and in His Son. The Bible is God's written word through which we encounter the truth about God and ourselves, which points us to Jesus. He is the living Word through whom we can know God as Father in a personal relationship. Jesus became God in human flesh and walked among us, as John declares in the opening of his gospel:

"The Word became flesh and made his dwelling among us. We have seen his glory, the glory of the one and only Son, who came from the Father, full of grace and truth' (John 1:14), 'No one has ever seen God, but the one and only Son, who is himself God and is in the closest relationship with the Father, has made him known." (John 1:18)

Jesus as the living Word of God goes beyond any previous understanding or revelation about God and His working, as Jesus is the fullest revelation of God given to humankind. This is most fully seen in His incarnation that became human, an unprecedented and unique act of God.

Bradley Jersak, in his book *'A More Christlike God,'* says that the incarnation of Jesus does not just refer to when Jesus came, but His whole life and death as revealing God to us. *'The incarnation refers to the whole life of Jesus and to Jesus Himself. That is, Jesus is the incarnation of God.'*[7] We use the term 'incarnation' to refer to God embodying His being and likeness in the person of Jesus Christ. Only Jesus is the full and exact likeness of God. God is, therefore, exactly what we see in Jesus, hence Bradley's term *'Christlike'*.[8] This is what God was always like.

In coming as one of us, in His life, and in Jesus dying for us, Jesus has become the bridge for us to know God, in both our mind and our heart. He reveals God not just in abstract thought, but in personal relationship; just as the Father and the Son are in closest relationship, we can also come to know God intimately as Lord and Saviour, even more than Abraham and Moses did. This is only possible through Jesus, the one who can break down the barrier of sin, shame and guilt, the barrier that keeps us from God. Jesus Himself states in Matthew 11:27.

> *"All things have been committed to me by my Father. No one knows the Son except the Father, and no one knows the Father except the Son and those to whom the Son chooses to reveal him."*

And in Matthew 26:28,

> *"This is my blood of the covenant, which is poured out for many for the forgiveness of sins."*

We see the fullness of what God is like in that He was willing to go to the Cross and die for us (see Chapter 3 for further discussion on what this means). Again, Bradley states, *'To look at the*

---

[7] Bradley Jersak, *A More Christlike God*, (Pasadena, CA: Plain Truth Ministries, 2015), p. 9.

[8] Jersak, *A More Christlike God* p. 81-84.

Cross is to look at God'.[9] The point here being that we see the inner life of the deity in its sharpest focus when we look at the Cross, at God Crucified. The more we meditate on the Cross, the more clearly we can see what God is like in His self-giving, *'kenotic'* love. 'The Cross reflects the true, *kenotic* and cruciform nature of God.'[10] (Jersak uses the term 'kenotic' based on the Greek text of Philippians 2:6, which is essentially God's self-giving love.)

It is when we believe in Jesus for the forgiveness of sins that we come to know God and receive eternal life in His name. When we do, we experience God's grace, forgiveness and truth which came fully in Jesus, who is the greater revelation of God's character first revealed to Moses (Exodus 34:6-7). There is a strong connection between God's revealed character to Moses, and revealed in Jesus (John 1:14), with the repetition of language: faithfulness/truth, compassion/grace, and God's glory, shows that Jesus is the exact likeness of God. The proclamation of Jesus in John 1:1-18 is the *'equivalent of the proclamation of God's character to Israel, the coming of Jesus full of grace and truth being evidence of his glory'.*[11]

When we have experienced God's grace and forgiveness, this should then inspire us to get to know God more. This we do through reading God's word, through prayer, and through fellowship and worshipping God with other Christians. As it says in 2 Peter 3:18:

> *"Grow in the grace and knowledge of our Lord and Saviour Jesus Christ."*

---

[9] Jersak, *A More Christlike God* p. 103.
[10] Jersak, *A More Christlike God* p. 179.
[11] Andrew Lincoln, *The Gospel According to St. John*, (Peabody, MA: Hendrickson Publishers, 2005), p. 106.

The context here is to turn away from the sinful ways in our life and from the godless ways of the world, and seek to learn and grow in the ways and knowledge of the Lord.

"'Make every effort to be found spotless, blameless and at peace with him. Bear in mind that our Lord's patience means salvation." (2 Peter 3:14-15)

Knowing God and having the hope of eternal life is a completely undeserved privilege and should motivate us to live in God's ways and to get to know Him more. This is discipleship, built on a relationship with God, not simply obedience to rules or mental consent, although these should stem from our relationship with God. In fact, the essence of eternal life is not just life forever, it begins in this life in knowing Jesus and the Father, *"Now this is eternal life: that they know you, the only true God, and Jesus Christ, whom you have sent"* (John 17:3). So, we come to know God through our Lord and Saviour Jesus Christ, and the gift of the Holy Spirit whom God gives to live within us. We will see more about this in the following chapter. Jesus is the one who reveals the fullness of God to us; His grace, His truth, and His glory.

Chapter 3. Jesus, the only Saviour

As we saw in Chapter 1, Jesus is described as the only Saviour of humanity, just as the God of Israel. In Chapter 2, we saw that the revelation of God to humanity is intrinsically connected to what God does for humanity, supremely in Jesus Christ. God's identity, '*is not simply revealed but enacted in the event of salvation for the world*'.[12] It is through the saving work of God in Jesus that He is most fully revealed and able to be known, as 'Saviour'. The term 'salvation' is key to understanding the importance of Jesus's deity, which we will explore in this chapter.

So, let us consider what the Bible means by salvation and how that relates to Jesus, as God, being the only Saviour of the world.

a) Salvation in Jesus alone

When the angel announced the birth of Jesus to the shepherds, he said:

> "*Today in the town of David a Saviour has been born to you; he is the Messiah, the Lord.*" (Luke 2:11)

This is described as a message of great joy for all the people (2:10). As the angel told Joseph at the birth of Jesus, Mary "*…will give birth to a son, and you are to give him the name Jesus, because he will save his people from their sins*" (Matthew 1:21). This is why His name is to be Jesus, because it means 'God saves'.

---

[12] Richard Bauckham, *Jesus and The God of Israel: God Crucified and Other Studies on The New Testament's Christology of Divine Identity*, (Milton Keynes: Paternoster, 2008), p. 50.

We saw above how Jesus shares in the identity of the only God, to whom alone every knee will bow (Philippians 2:10-11, alluding to Isaiah 45:23). In the verses in Isaiah just before this, we read.

"And there is no God apart from me, a righteous God and a Saviour; there is none but me." (Isaiah 45:21)

This passage declares there is no other Saviour than the LORD, the God of Israel. Jesus now takes up this role as the only God who can save people.

"Salvation is found in no one else, for there is no other name under heaven given to humankind by which we must be saved." (Acts 4:12)

To understand what this salvation means, let us then see what it meant for God to be Saviour in the Old Testament, and how this relates to what it means for Jesus to be Saviour.

b) Redemption and rescue

The most foundational action of God in saving people in the Old Testament is His redeeming of the Israelites out of slavery in Egypt. This not only set Israel on the path to be its own nation in a covenant relationship with God from that point onwards, but it also unsurprisingly became the most referenced act of God in the Old Testament. Future generations looked back on this monumental event, in expectation of God to similarly aid His people in their present. Psalm 106:4-10 is just one example where the psalmist reflects on God's redemption in the past, despite the sins of the Israelites, giving confidence for God's aid in their present.

"Remember me, Lord, when you show favour to your people, come to my aid when you save them, that I may enjoy the prosperity of your chosen ones, that I may share in the joy of your nation and join your inheritance in giving praise.

We have sinned, even as our ancestors did; we have done wrong and acted wickedly. When our ancestors were in Egypt, they gave no thought to your miracles; they did not remember your many kindnesses, and they rebelled by the sea, the Red Sea. Yet he saved them for his name's sake, to make his mighty power known. He rebuked the Red Sea, and it dried up; he led them through the depths as through a desert. He saved them from the hand of the foe; from the hand of the enemy he redeemed them."

God saved His people from slavery and brought them into a place of prosperity and covenant relation with Him, even though the Israelites failed to live up to God's Law in the covenant. This was God's grace to redeem them, which they never deserved. This itself shows God's mercy and intent to save people rather than condemn them, and results in His glory because of His grace and wonderful deeds. This gave God's people confidence that He could and would act again to save His people in other situations of trouble (although sometimes this was presumed even when God said they would face judgement because of persistent sin). [13] What God did in the Exodus was revealing as to His nature to save, deliver and redeem, whether the needy, oppressed, or enslaved. God is called Saviour, Deliverer and Redeemer many times in the Old Testament (e.g. Psalm 18:2; Isaiah 49:26). It is something God does even though it is undeserved.

We also see that King David recalls how God saved him from his enemies, from the threat of death from Saul in particular (2 Samuel 22:1-4). He cried out to God (22:7), who rescued him from a powerful enemy, who supported him in the day of disaster, bringing him into a spacious place (22:18-20). David praises the LORD who saves the humble (22:28), and who shields those who take refuge in Him (22:31). David acknowledged the LORD is his

---

[13] E.g. Jeremiah 6:14-15.

Rock – One who is unshakable, solid, dependable, providing a firm foundation to stand on. He is worthy of praise (22:47, 50). The important thing David did was that he cried out to God in his distress and trouble, and afterwards, he acknowledged how the LORD had helped him, even saving him from death at the hand of Saul.

This gives a precedent for us, that we can seek God's saving help in times of trouble, as One who rescues the oppressed and downtrodden. It does not necessarily mean He will immediately remove us from the situation, but because His nature is to save and help the needy. When we turn to Him in dependence and faith, He will come to our aid, sometimes in ways we do not expect. He can save us from the sins and evil of others, but we should remember there is no total escape from such things whilst we are in this broken and sinful world.

Because Jesus is fully divine and fully human, He alone can bridge the gap between humanity and God caused by sin (see below). Thus, it is through Jesus we can approach God's throne of grace to find help in our time of need, and it is because Jesus experienced human life that He can sympathise with our weakness (Hebrews 4:14-16). Moses mediated between God and Israel in the Exodus, but not as an eternal mediator through whom Israel prayed.

Israel's exodus from Egypt is a powerful witness of how God similarly redeems us out of spiritual slavery, i.e. 'sin'. Romans 3:24 says:

> *"All are justified freely by his grace through the redemption that came by Christ Jesus."*

Redemption in the New Testament strongly overlaps with forgiveness of sins and being justified, made right with God, which is found only in Christ Jesus. This is only possible because Jesus was the perfect sacrifice for our sins (3:25), which no mere man or angel could achieve.

As Christopher Wright notes, this does not negate the reality or lessen the importance of the Exodus story as a historical saving act of God; of what that meant for Israel, or what it can mean for us as political, economic, social and spiritual deliverance.[14] The Exodus demonstrates God's power and victory over evil in His judgement on Pharaoh and the 'gods of Egypt' (Exodus 12:12). Likewise, the New Testament decares how after the Father raised Jesus from the dead, He also raised Him up to sit at His right hand, above all rule, authority, power and dominion, in this age and the age to come, as head over all things (Ephesians 1:20-22). This speaks to the deity of Jesus, who is seated at God's right hand and has power over all things (also see Colossians 1:15-20). It is in Jesus, therefore, that there is ultimate victory over evil, which includes sin and even death. This is only possible if Jesus has this divine standing, which is for the sake of the church (Ephesians 1:23), that is, all who believe in Him as Lord and Saviour.

In the Old Testament, God was seen as the Saviour of His people Israel, but that did not prevent other people from calling out to the LORD. There was some awareness that God was Saviour of other nations, *"...the hope of all the ends of the earth"* (Psalm 65:5). But it was when God came in Jesus that His salvation was displayed and made available to all peoples and nations, *"...we have seen and testify that the Father has sent his Son to be the Saviour of the world"* (1 John 4:14). As such it is in Jesus that we now call on God to rescue us, to save us. This certainly includes rescue from trouble and evil, but God's primary act of salvation, as alluded to above, is in saving people from their sins.

---

[14] Christopher. J. H. Wright, *Knowing God Through The Old Testament*, (Downers Grove, IVP, 2019), p.33.

c) Forgiveness of sins

The theme of 'forgiveness of sins' is indeed prominent in the New Testament, but we should not think it is a solely New Testament concept. For example, we see in Psalm 79:9:

> *"Help us, God our Saviour, for the glory of your name; deliver us and forgive our sins for your name's sake."*

Israel would be encouraged to return to God and pray for forgiveness in recognition of their sin, in breaking the covenant by trusting and worshipping other gods.

> *"'Say to him: 'Forgive all our sins and receive us graciously, that we may offer the fruit of our lips…" (Hosea 14:2)*

We see shortly after the exodus, when Moses was on the mountain for 40 days with God, that Israel turned to worship a false God. The Israelites did not know where Moses had ended up and so made a golden calf to lead them and worshipped it instead of the LORD, who had saved them. Moses interceded for Israel, and God forgave their sins, even though there was a measure of judgement (Exodus 32). It is God's nature and heart to forgive, but He will bring judgement if people refuse to turn from evil.

> *"The LORD, the LORD, the compassionate and gracious God, slow to anger, abounding in love and faithfulness, maintaining love to thousands, and forgiving wickedness, rebellion and sin. Yet he does not leave the guilty unpunished…" (Exodus 34:6-7)*

For this reason, God compels people to repent, to turn from their evil ways and follow His ways, so they may live.

> *"As surely as I live, declares the Sovereign LORD, I take no pleasure in the death of the wicked, but rather that they turn from their ways and live. Turn! Turn from your evil ways!" (Ezekiel 33:11)*

When we turn to the New Testament, we see that in Jesus, repentance of sins is to be preached to all nations (Luke 24:47). Repentance simply means turning from a life apart from God, to follow God's ways. It is because Jesus is both divine and human that in Him alone can there be complete forgiveness of sins. When Jesus healed and forgave the paralysed man in Mark 2 / Luke 5, the Pharisees acknowledged that only God can forgive sins. Jesus proved He had the authority to forgive sins by healing the man.

As noted above, the theme of redemption overlaps with the forgiveness of sins numerous times in the New Testament. This reaches a pinnacle when Jesus gave His life as a ransom (Mark 10:45). By His death, He brings us out of slavery to sin and death by His blood, so we no longer remain under God's eternal judgement for our sins. One of the key battles in the Exodus narrative is God acting to bring His enslaved people to Himself, out from under the oppressive hand of Pharaoh, who sought to keep the Israelites as His slaves. Just as God did for Israel, Jesus similarly rescues us from the power of Satan, the oppressor, who would keep us in bondage to sin and death and keep us from God. This is the main thrust of Jesus' universal saving work and is necessary for all people in order to be brought back to God. Because Jesus is God, He alone can forgive our sins and redeem us, as the only One without sin. He is humanity's only Saviour.

Many people today struggle with the concept of sin, but according to Alan Mann, are more likely to understand shame: feeling self-diminished, feeling defiled, unwanted, not good enough, and self-judged.[15] This is also seen in the search for intimacy in relationships, which eludes so many.[16] This can be seen in the New Testament in reconciliation with God, being brought back to God in

---

[15] Alan Mann, *Atonement for a Sinless Society*, (Cambridge: James Clark & Co., 2016), p. 24-25.

[16] Mann, *Atonement*, p. 28.

a positive relationship with Him. Again, this overlaps with the themes of redemption and forgiveness.

d) Reconciliation and relationship with God

In Romans 5, Paul explains that in Christ we are reconciled to God, made at peace with Him through the death of Christ (5:1-11), which is God's free gift of grace to us (5:15-21). In Romans 6, Paul emphasises the call for Christians to live a new life, not thinking God's grace is an excuse to keep sinning (6:1-4). This was precisely the mistake the presumptuous Israelites made when they believed God would always protect them, regardless of how they were living. If we have truly encountered God's grace and forgiveness, we should not want to keep living in opposition to Him. Once we understand our need for reconciliation with God through Jesus, we must also understand the Christian teaching of sin and the need to change, and repentance from the heart. The whole idea of reconciliation is about a relationship with God, not just a free pardon for sin without any willingness to change. Following Romans 6:1-4, we read in 6:5-7:

> *"For if we have been united with him in a death like his, we will certainly also be united with him in a resurrection like his. For we know that our old self was crucified with him so that the body ruled by sin might be done away with [or: rendered powerless], that we should no longer be slaves to sin – because anyone who has died has been set free from sin."*

This circles back to the theme of redemption, being set free. Salvation in Jesus is a whole package with many facets; none are supreme at the exclusion of the others. If we have been joined to Christ by turning away from sin, letting Christ take our sin and guilt on the Cross, we are also joined to Christ in His resurrection, meaning we too will be raised with Him and can live a new life. This is true even now, being under God's grace, rather than submitting to the desires of the sinful nature and being under its power. Romans 8:23 speaks of *"...the redemption of our bodies..."*, highlighting too the future dimension of our bodily resurrection in the age to come.

In Christ, we have died to our old self and are set free to live for God. Previously, this was not possible, as we were *'slaves to sin'*. Just as the Israelites could not free themselves from slavery in Egypt, so we cannot free ourselves from slavery and bondage to sin. It is only by the saving grace and power of God in Jesus Christ, who died to break the power of sin over us and rose from the dead to enable us to live for God. Even though we still sin in this life, yet we can still live for God, being reconciled to God, being freed to know Him and live under His grace. In Christ, we have God's power to resist the sinful nature that opposes God and therefore live to please Him through the gift of the Holy Spirit, whom He gives to aid us in the Christian life.

When we see Jesus face to face, then we will be without sin completely, just as He is (1 John 3:2). We are therefore to crucify the sinful nature, meaning we are to do away with those things that hinder our relationship with God. By doing so we render our sinful desires powerless to control us as they once did, because we are also seated with Christ in the heavenly realms (Ephesians 2:6). This simply means we have power to overcome temptations (which stems from a broken relationship with God) and any evil forces, or addictions that would keep us in a life of sin, because of Jesus's power and His divine standing. It does not mean it will be quick and easy, as we are still in a spiritual battle. Jesus sets us free to live a new life as *"...slaves of righteousness..."*, which leads to holiness in life (Romans 6:16-23).

So, through faith in Christ, He takes our sin, and we are credited with His righteousness (Romans 4:22-25). We are now in right standing with God (5:1) and have a restored relationship with God in Jesus Christ. To be under God's grace is a place of blessing; it is freedom from the control of sin, not to do what we want, but freedom to now live for righteousness. Freedom to do whatever we want is in fact, submitting to the sinful nature, but the end result of these two paths could not be more different. Repentance should similarly be seen positively, because it brings us into life rather than death. The gift of forgiveness and eternal life is only possible because of the saving work of Jesus, and because Jesus is divine, He can share the eternal life of God with us.

e) Holiness and eternal life

Paul tells us in Romans 6:18 that slavery to sin leads to death, whilst slavery to righteousness leads to holiness and eternal life. Being slaves to sin or submitting simply to whatever we want often results in suffering or oppression of others, even if not directly, as it is self-centred. It is not healthy for us to live that way. But even worse, what we get from that as our just payment is death (Romans 3:23, 6:23). This is why we die, because of our inherent sinful nature which was the result of Adam's sin and disobedience to God (Romans 5:12). But it is also a spiritual death, separation from God, not knowing God. This is our natural position, and unless God took the initiative in Jesus, we could not know Him or be made spiritually alive. Paul sums this up nicely in Ephesians 2:3-5:

> *"All of us also lived among them at one time, gratifying the cravings of our sinful nature and following its desires and thoughts. Like the rest, we were by nature deserving of wrath. But because of his great love for us, God, who is rich in mercy, made us alive with Christ even when we were dead in transgressions—it is by grace you have been saved."*

Something that is dead cannot make itself alive again. Only in Jesus can we be made spiritually alive, to know God and have the hope of eternal life. Yes, we will still die physically (unless Christ comes back first), but because we are joined to Christ, we will also be physically raised with a new body that cannot die (1 Corinthians 15:42-44). This is the end result of being 'slaves to righteousness'. It is not about trying to follow rules; it is about a new relationship with Jesus as our God, who has given us new life, that we may delight in Him, find blessing, and be a blessing to others in His name. This is basically the essence of being holy. Peter describes this as *"...participation in the divine nature..."* (2 Peter 1:4). Not that we become divine, but we become like God's character in Jesus, sharing in His divine life and eternal goodness.

When the Israelites were delivered from slavery in Egypt, it was not so they could just live how they wanted, it was so they could know God, worship Him, learn what it means to be His people, follow His ways, and be a blessing to others, showing the nations a new and better life. This is a picture of the redemption and new life we now have in Jesus.

When the New Testament talks about life, it is nearly always referring to the spiritual aspect of a relationship with God, which we can know now and will fully know in the age to come. John's gospel often uses the term 'Eternal life'; it is a quality of life, an abundance not just 'everlasting' in a sense of time. Eternal life is only possible in Jesus because in Him is the true life for which God intended for us. Jesus Himself is God and thus has the divine life in Him.

"In Him was life, and that life was the light of all people."
(John 1:4)

And as Jesus says in John 11:25:

"I am the resurrection and the life. The one who believes in me will live, even though they die."

The essence of this life is knowing God (17:3), is governed by righteousness, and is truly life to the full (10:10), which at present we have but a foretaste.

Salvation and eternal life depend on God's grace and God's promise, which are brought to fulfilment in Jesus. As a result, trusting in anyone or anything else cannot save us from our sins and bring us into eternal life. When the Israelites were under threat from the Babylonians, hundreds of years after the Exodus, God reminded them time and time again that they cannot rely on anything else to save them (e.g. Isaiah 31). We can only rely on Jesus for salvation. He alone is God our Saviour (Titus 2:13). Jesus, being God, became God crucified for us, because only He was without sin and therefore able to deal with our sin. This is why the Father sent the Son to save the world and bring back to God all who will turn to and rely on Him.

That God should come to save us is remarkable. A huge implication of that is worth our attention in the next chapter: that God suffered, becoming the crucified God.

Chapter 4. Jesus, the suffering God

As we already stated, when Jesus came to dwell amongst us, He did not just come to teach us God's ways; He came to die to take our sins upon Himself so we might have eternal life. It is impossible for us to imagine the extent of the suffering to which Jesus went in His crucifixion. This is not a morbid or sadistic endeavour; it shows us the magnitude of the consequences of our sin, the magnitude of what it cost God to redeem us, and the magnitude of His love and grace towards us to bring us into His kingdom.

The suffering of Jesus was not limited to just His crucifixion, although this is of primary importance. There are two relevant points here: Firstly, His dwelling among us as a human being shows us something about God's identification with us in suffering. This, secondly, helps us to see how we might begin to understand more broadly the common question of how a good and all-powerful God could allow so much suffering in the world. God's suffering for our sinfulness and the effects in this world were far deeper than physical suffering. For the divine being could ensure His actions reached into the depths of the problem of suffering, He had to become a human being. Only then could He understand our situations (Hebrews 4:16) and bring redemption for the whole cosmos. So, in this chapter, we proceed to understand that suffering and how God deals with it.

a) Jesus suffered for us

All four gospels dedicate a significant portion of their narrative to Jesus' last week of His ministry, culminating in His unjust trial by the religious authorities and His agonising crucifixion by the Romans. All four gospels conclude with the accounts of Jesus' resurrection and deliverance from death three days later. His resurrection in no way detracts from what Jesus went through in order to save us and open the door for us to eternal life with Him. John, in his gospel, tells us that even after Jesus was raised from the dead, He still bore the marks of His crucifixion. Thomas said he would not believe unless he saw the marks of His crucifixion. So, Jesus said to Thomas, *"Put your finger here; see my hands. Reach out your hand and put it into my side. Stop doubting and believe."* (John 20:27). He presumably took those scars into the ascended position He now has besides God the Father.

Jesus knew He would have to die. He referred to this to His disciples on at least three occasions, and that He would then be raised to life again on the third day (e.g. Mark 8:31; 9:30; 10:32), He knew it was Judas Iscariot who would betray Him (John 6:71). The night before His crucifixion, after He ate the Last Supper with His disciples (which was the Passover meal, connecting Jesus' pending death to the Exodus account of God's redemption of Israel out of Egypt), Jesus went to the Garden of Gethsemane with His disciples to pray. Jesus spent those night hours in prayer, wrestling with the horror He was about to endure.

> *"He took Peter, James and John along with him, and he began to be deeply distressed and troubled. 'My soul is overwhelmed with sorrow to the point of death,' he said to them. 'Stay here and keep watch.' Going a little farther, he fell to the ground and prayed that if possible the hour might pass from him. 'Abba, Father,' he said, 'everything is possible for you. Take this cup from me. Yet not what I will, but what you will."* (Mark 14:33-36)

He was so distressed, His sweat was like drops of blood (Luke 22:43). Jesus was distressed at the reality of what was about to happen to Him. Jesus was completely faithful to the Father, having no sin, and knew there was no other way to bring salvation to humanity; He had already told His disciples what must happen. He was wrestling with the distress of what He knew He would face, being completely human like us. Just because Jesus is God, He was in no way immune to the pain and horror of His crucifixion; it was very real for Him. This shows us the reality of His humanity as God with us, not just with us in coming to earth, but also in the real experiences we go through as human beings.

His submission to the Father's will was not something He was unwilling to do, as if the Father was forcing Him to do this like some cosmic child abuse. No! Jesus willingly went to the cross because of His love for us and His pleasure to do His Father's will. John makes it clear through what He records Jesus saying,

"No one takes [my life] from me, but I lay it down of my own accord." (John 10:18), and

"My food… is to do the will of him who sent me and to finish his work." (John 4:34)

As God the Son, Jesus came to do the work of salvation, which was the Father's will and plan even before Creation. It was because of His great love for us that Jesus went to the cross, suffering brutal torture with 39 lashes (John 19:1), having to carry His own cross, having nails driven through His hands and feet, and left hanging on the cross for 6 hours until He eventually died. The Romans and their predecessors had long devised one of the most horrific ways to torture and kill someone, dragging out the pain, as well as public shame and mockery. When you read the gospel accounts and some of the prophecies about the suffering and death of the Messiah (e.g. Psalm 22:1-18; Isaiah 53:3-9), you get a sense of some of what Jesus went through for us.

It was more than just physical suffering for Jesus, though, because He had to bear the sins of the world upon His shoulders (1 Peter 2:24). Such spiritual suffering is incomprehensible. God the

Son was separated from God the Father (Matthew 27:46) whom He had always been in closest relationship with (Matthew 11:27 and John 1:18, 5:19). It was a complete separation as He bore our judgement of sin upon Himself (cf. 2 Cor.5:21 - He became sin), dying an excruciating death.

> *"For God so loved the world that he gave his one and only Son, that whoever believes in him shall not perish but have eternal life."* (John 3:16)

Jesus also suffered in that He wept for the brokenness and godlessness of the world around Him. He was deeply troubled and wept over the death of His friend Lazarus (John 11:33-35), even though He was going to raise Him from the dead. It signifies His pain in the suffering that death causes in our present world. He also wept over Jerusalem because it had rejected God's coming and salvation for them, and the suffering it would soon face in its destruction by the Romans as a result (Luke 19:41-44).

All this to say, then, that God certainly experienced suffering in the person of Jesus, even more than probably most of us, especially in His crucifixion. As God has joined Himself to our suffering as the divine human, this then becomes crucial to how God deals with the problem of suffering in the world and the hope that brings.

b) God and the problem of suffering

We have seen how God suffered as one of us as the man Jesus, and how He suffered for us to take away our sin. This can lead us to consider why there is so much suffering in the world to begin with, and what God has done about it, proving His love for humanity and the world. Why does God not just take it away, though? It is a question many of us wrestle with, a question that we can honestly bring to the Bible. Being full of real human experiences, the Bible can help provide us with a deeper perspective about suffering from the context of faith in Jesus, the one who suffered for us supremely on the cross. It is worth noting that we should not expect answers to why every single thing in life happens, but the perspective the Bible gives us can provide real comfort and hope; suffering need not be an obstacle to faith in a loving, all-powerful God.

Firstly, the fact that God suffered with us and for us in Jesus shows He is not disconnected from the suffering of the world, He has become part of it in Jesus. This is expressed well in 'The Long Silence Poem' (author unknown).[17] It's a helpful reflection that shows the necessity of God coming down in Jesus to partake in our suffering.

> *"At the end of time, billions of people were seated on a great plain before God's throne. Most shrank back from the brilliant light before them. But some groups near the front talked heatedly, not cringing with cringing shame - but with belligerence.*
>
> *'Can God judge us? How can He know about suffering?', snapped a pert young brunette. She ripped open a sleeve to reveal a tattooed number from a Nazi concentration camp. 'We endured terror ... beatings ... torture ... death!' ...*
>
> *In another crowd there was a pregnant schoolgirl with sullen eyes: 'Why should I suffer?' she murmured. 'It wasn't my fault.' Far out across the plain were hundreds of such groups. Each had a complaint against God for the evil and suffering He had permitted in His world.*
>
> *How lucky God was to live in Heaven, where all was sweetness and light. Where there was no weeping or fear, no hunger or hatred. What did God know of all that man had been forced to*

---

[17] https://www.ldolphin.org/silence.html

endure in this world? For God leads a pretty sheltered life, they said."

"So each of these groups sent forth their leader, chosen because he had suffered the most. A Jew, a negro, a person from Hiroshima, a horribly deformed arthritic, a thalidomide child. In the centre of the vast plain, they consulted with each other. At last they were ready to present their case. It was rather clever.

Before God could be qualified to be their judge, He must endure what they had endured. Their decision was that God should be sentenced to live on earth as a man.

Let him be born a Jew. Let the legitimacy of his birth be doubted. Give him a work so difficult that even his family will think him out of his mind.

Let him be betrayed by his closest friends. Let him face false charges, be tried by a prejudiced jury and convicted by a cowardly judge. Let him be tortured.

At the last, let him see what it means to be terribly alone. Then let him die so there can be no doubt he died. Let there be a great host of witnesses to verify it.

As each leader announced his portion of the sentence, loud murmurs of approval went up from the throng of people assembled. When the last had finished pronouncing sentence, there was a long silence. No one uttered a word. No one moved.

For suddenly, all knew that God had already served His sentence."

Secondly, God has not just entered into our suffering; He has put steps in place to do something about it. These are seen in God's promises and actions, which are central to the plotline of God's redeeming love for the world in the biblical narrative. This was only possible because in His love, God joined Himself to our suffering, so as to redeem us and creation from it.

And thirdly, because God can identify with our suffering, He can draw near to us and provide comfort and strength through His promises and presence with us.

To help see this, let us consider why there is suffering and death in the world and how that shapes our perspective. In the most general sense, the reason is that after Adam and Eve sinned against God. God pronounced judgement on them, which separated them from His presence in paradise. Life, subsequent to that, became a struggle with toil, pain and death (Genesis 3:17-19). This was just on God's part. He created the world and gave life. There was no obligation for Him to do so, and as we have seen, God has to deal with sin; otherwise, He would not be just in putting things right. At least some of the time, this is seen in God giving people over to the consequences of their ways upon continuous rejection of God (i.e. Romans 1:18-25). The Bible illustrates how, after humans rebelled against God, things only got worse. Adam and Eve's son Cain murdered his brother (Genesis 4:8). The wickedness and sin have not changed since human beings first rebelled against God. The fact that God did not get rid of humanity, even in the Flood (Genesis 6-9), shows He is committed to us, although He knows we are sinful. God is committed to dealing with the suffering and sin in the world. The death and resurrection of Jesus are key to eventually putting an end to sin and death. Without the cross where Jesus died, God still remains distant to suffering, and without the resurrection of Jesus, there is no hope of an end to suffering or final justice for millions who have suffered unjustly.[18]

---

[18] John Lennox in *'Oxford Mathematician DESTROYS Atheism (15 Minute Brilliancy!)'* https://www.youtube.com/watch?v=VrIvwPConv0&list=WL&index=6 13:44 – 14:35. Accessed 9th January 2025.

A large amount of the suffering in the world can be attributed to the sin of people. James 3:16 tells us, *"...where you have envy and selfish ambition, there you find disorder and every evil practice."* This is the broad perspective on evil, and hence suffering, that the Bible reveals to us. It is so often rooted in the sinful human nature.[19] Quite often, there are human factors of evil or folly, such as direct actions that cause suffering, but also indirect such as building houses on flood plains, or inadequate systems of healthcare.

That is why, thirdly, the Cross is so important, because God in Jesus took on Himself the sins of the world, becoming part of our suffering whilst also opening the way for us to find forgiveness and hope amidst suffering. Forgiveness because we are all part of the problem and need God's saving grace, which in turn gives us assurance of hope in God's promises for us and the world. The resurrection shows that God has conquered evil and death, and if we trust in Jesus, we have the assurance of forgiveness and the hope of eternal life without suffering. As Dr. C. Fred Smith observes, *'Jürgen Moltmann sees the suffering of Christ as God's way of participating in our human despair, taking it into Himself, and replacing it with hope.'*[20] Because God plunged the depths of suffering in the cross and overcame it in His resurrection, we too have the hope to overcome in Jesus and His promise of the new creation.

Natural suffering likewise entered the human experience after Adam and Eve sinned. When disasters happen in this life, there are often many factors to why they occur. Let us be clear that the Bible does not say we suffer in a particular circumstance because it is God punishing us for some sin. Jesus challenged that

---

[19] See further on suffering and evil, 'Tim Keller on Suffering and Evil, https://billmuehlenberg.com/2023/06/23/tim-keller-on-suffering-and-evil/.'

[20] The Suffering of Christ on the Cross in the Theology of Jürgen Moltmann. https://urnottheonlyone.com/2017/07/11/the-suffering-of-christ-on-the-cross-in-the-theology-of-jurgen-moltmann/

perspective on several occasions (Luke 13:1-5; John 9:1-3). Suffering is part of our experience because we live in a fallen and sinful world. Jesus was the only one ever without sin, yet He suffered during His life, as well as in the most horrific way in His death. He was deeply troubled and wept over His friend Lazarus, who had died, and the pain that death causes in the world (John 11:33-36). God is concerned about those who are oppressed and afflicted (e.g. Exodus 2:23-25). Notice what it says in Luke 4:18-19, often referred to as Jesus' mission manifesto, how there is an emphasis on delivering people from suffering and oppression.

> *"The Spirit of the Lord is on me, because he has anointed me to proclaim good news to the poor. He has sent me to proclaim freedom for the prisoners and recovery of sight for the blind, to set the oppressed free, to proclaim the year of the Lord's favour."*

God is very much concerned about the suffering we go through. The Bible does not say God will take away all our suffering in this life if we just believe enough, live good enough lives, or give enough money to the church. No! Certainly, God can and does heal people even in our day. There is much which could be said about why God does not heal some people and others He does. Jesus, in His ministry, healed many, even those who did not ask or did not give thanks (Luke 17:11-19). But even in the Bible, there were limited times when God performed miracles and healings to a large degree. God did many signs and wonders through the apostles in the early church and even beyond to show the inauguration of God's kingdom as a result of the resurrection. This may have something to do with miracles authenticating God's message of salvation and the authoritative claims of Jesus (e.g. Mark 2:1-12).

What the Bible does tell us for sure is that God comforts us in our hardships. Having suffered as one of us in Jesus, He is more than able to identify with our suffering, help us in it, and draw near to us. Even when we feel alone, God is still there for us and will see us through. Even Jesus felt alone on the Cross (Matthew 27:45), but He knew He could rely on His Father and commit Himself wholly to Him (Luke 23:46).

Fourthly, He also uses our suffering to even bring about good. This does not mean it is good to suffer, but that God is able to bring good out of our suffering. Whether or not God heals or delivers us from suffering, we ought to trust God. He gives us comfort, strength, hope, and training through the hardships we go through. Consider the following passages:

> *"For we do not have a high priest who is unable to feel sympathy for our weaknesses, but we have one who has been tempted in every way, just as we are – yet he did not sin. Let us then approach God's throne of grace with confidence, so that we may receive mercy and find grace to help us in our time of need." (Hebrews 4:15-16)*

> *"Praise be to the God and Father of our Lord Jesus Christ, the Father of compassion and the God of all comfort, who comforts us in all our troubles, so that we can comfort those in any trouble with the comfort we ourselves receive from God. For just as we share abundantly in the sufferings of Christ, so also our comfort abounds through Christ." (2 Corinthians 1:3-5)*

> *"…though now for a little while you may have had to suffer grief in all kinds of trials. These have come so that the proven genuineness of your faith – of greater worth than gold, which perishes even though refined by fire – may result in praise, glory and honour when Jesus Christ is revealed." (1 Peter 1:6b-7)*

On this last passage, we should note that God can and does use our trials and hardships that we go through to strengthen us in faith and character. Like being refined through fire, it is not a pleasant experience, but God uses it for our spiritual good, and will result in praise, glory and honour to Him. This will especially be the case when Jesus Christ is revealed. Presently, we may not be able to see how God is bringing good out of a situation, but one day we will see how He used the trials we have gone through to bring about good in other ways. Again, this does not mean God allows terrible things to happen because He thinks they are good, or for some 'higher purpose' which can make a mockery of the tragedies and horrors some people face. God may be all-powerful, but there is a freedom to natural law and human will in God's creation, which He subjected Himself to in Jesus, especially at the Cross.[21] God grieves with us and in Jesus has promised that one day all things will be set right. Without a suffering and loving God, which we see in Jesus, there is no real comfort or justice.

As noted above, we should not think God is punishing us when life gets tough. God uses hardships to train and disciple us because He loves us and wants us to be brought to maturity (Hebrews 12:6-10). *"No discipline seems pleasant at the time, but painful. Later on, however, it produces a harvest of righteousness and peace for those who have been trained by it"* (12:11). If there is blatant sin in our life, God will seek to bring that to our attention and discipline us so we will get rid of that sin. We see this especially through the challenges of the Old Testament prophets to sinful Israel. His discipline is always as a perfect loving Father for our good and maturity, and not to be confused with abusive punishment!

As the passage noted in 2 Corinthians reminds us, God is able to use the hardships we go through to enable us to help others. Comfort in the Bible is not just helping someone feel better, it has a sense of strengthening, like a warrior for battle or an athlete for the games. God can also use our hardships to bring about good in other

---

[21] Bradley Jersak, *A More Christlike God*, (Plain Truth Ministries, Pasadena, 2015), p. 171-72.

ways. In Genesis 37-50, we read the story of Joseph, how he was sold into slavery by his brothers, ended up as a slave in Egypt, was falsely accused and imprisoned for 2 years. But then God raised him up to be the second highest in all Egypt, in order to save many from a terrible famine. After he was reconciled to his brothers and after his father died, his brothers were afraid Jospeh would pay them back for selling him into slavery, but Joseph told them, *"You intended to harm me, but God intended it for good to accomplish what is now being done, the saving of many lives"* (Genesis 50:20). Joseph clearly had a divine perspective on what he had gone through. He realised God allowed him to be sold into slavery so he could save many lives. This may have taken him time, but that is an example of how we can approach our trials. We can see our lives as contributing to bringing God's goodness and kingdom here on earth.

In all then, yes, terrible things do happen, and we should not make light of that. Let us not think that God has planned to make that happen like fate! It was Joseph's brothers who were guilty of sin, but God brought about much good despite the wicked act of his brothers. God is able to work good in any situation for those who love Him, for those who are His (Romans 8:28). Of course, if certain things did not happen, that would be better. But we cannot live in regret or ifs and buts, we have to live with hope and trust in God, and in the end to know He will put all wrongs right and wipe away every tear, and destroy all death and evil (Revelation 21:4). Because God suffered with us and for us in His Son, He knows how to help us in our time of need, and we can hold fast to His promises in the life to come for those who hold fast to Jesus Christ in the present, who gives us strength, will never forsake us, and brings us to maturity in His grace, salvation and hope.

Chapter 5. Jesus, the eternal and supreme Lord

We have already seen in chapter 1 the clear declaration that Jesus is Lord, which equates to His divine status. There are several huge implications of this truth which affect our view of the world in the present, our hope for the world in the future, and our relationship with Jesus, as individuals and the church. There are four main themes I wish to explore, which will help us see the importance of this lordship of Jesus: that He is 'King of kings and Lord of lords', is to be worshipped by all, is to be proclaimed by the church, and is to be followed as our Lord.

a) King of kings and Lord of lords

The phrase *"King of kings and Lord of lords"* appears three times in the New Testament (1 Timothy 6:15; Revelation 17:14; 19:16). It clearly denotes the supreme nature of God's rule above all other rulers, *"the only Ruler"* (1 Timothy 6:15). All three uses are in the context of the return of Christ to judge the world. No other kings or rulers, or spiritual forces of evil, will be able to stand against Jesus or avoid His judgement. We see the exalted place of Jesus, for example, in Ephesians 1:17-23.

> *"I keep asking that the God of our Lord Jesus Christ, the glorious Father, may give you the Spirit of wisdom and revelation, so that you may know him better. I pray that the eyes of your heart may be enlightened in order that you may know the hope to which he has called you, the riches of his glorious inheritance in his holy people, and his incomparably great power for us who believe. That power is the same as the mighty strength he exerted when he raised Christ from the dead and seated him at his right hand*

in the heavenly realms, far above all rule and authority, power and dominion, and every name that is invoked, not only in the present age but also in the one to come. And God placed all things under his feet and appointed him to be head over everything for the church, which is his body, the fullness of him who fills everything in every way."

There is much depth and theological reflection we could tease out of this passage, but for our purpose, I want to bring out four things from this powerful and profound scripture: that Jesus has authority at God's right hand, over the church, over evil forces, and over our lives.

Firstly, we see that after His resurrection, *Jesus was given the place of authority at the right hand of His Father on His heavenly throne.* To be at someone's right hand is the ultimate place of authority in ancient and biblical thought. To be sure, Jesus was always with the Father in glory until He came to earth (John 17:5). His saving work on the cross and His resurrection have brought Him victory over the spiritual forces of evil and over death itself. This is not to say He was not Lord prior to His resurrection – in sharing in the divine identity of the LORD, the God of Israel. His resurrection proved to the world His status as 'our Lord' and 'Son of God' (Romans 1:4). As we shall see below, the honour of worship Jesus deserves is linked to His eternal divine status, not something He later received.

As alluded to in the Ephesians passage, the authority of Jesus is supreme in both this age and the age to come. We noted the context of the Revelation passage about the coming of Christ to judge the world, especially Revelation chapters 19-20. The Father appointed Jesus to judge the living and the dead (Acts 10:42), to whom all are accountable (1 Peter 4:5). All will recognise His divine authority and eternal lordship on that day (Philippians 2:10-11).

Secondly, *Jesus as Lord has authority over the church.* This means He is the head of the church (see Colossians 1:18), a position which no one else can rightfully claim. That does not mean there are to be no church leaders; several of the New Testament letters discuss the role of leaders in the church.[22] Rather, all within the church are subject to the authority of Jesus. This includes how the church is run and how it represents Jesus as ambassadors of God's kingdom (2 Corinthians 5:20): with integrity of life, in line with the teaching of Scripture, and God's will and purposes rather than our own agendas. This requires churches and leaders to always pray for God's leading, otherwise they can easily go astray or become unproductive in the work of God's kingdom. Any role within the church should be taken with reverence for the authority and will of God, knowing we are accountable to Jesus as the head over all things. The same could also be said about any Christian in a worldly place of authority. One should always seek to do what is right according to God's word and acknowledge their accountability to Jesus for how they use their authority and witness to the gospel. The lordship of Jesus demands both communal and individual acknowledgement of our accountability to Him.

Thirdly, *Jesus has authority over all spiritual forces.* The Bible is clear that there are other spiritual beings, such as angels and demons, which are at work behind the visible world (e.g. Ephesians 6:12; Job 1:6-12; Daniel 10:12-14). These have certain authority and limitations under God's sovereignty. Since Jesus is seated in the place of highest authority on God's throne, we as the church ought to pray and seek His will with all kinds of prayers and petitions (Ephesians 6:18), which is an essential part of our spiritual armour along with the word of God to confront forces of evil (Ephesians 6:10-18). We are also told to pray for those in authority (1 Timothy

---

[22] E.g. 1 Timothy; Titus; 1 Peter 5.

2:1-4) that God's kingdom will come on earth as in heaven (Matthew 6:10).

This also means we should not dabble with other spiritual forces and practices as they are an affront to God (Isaiah 8:19-22). We must trust in Christ as the one with supreme lordship and instead receive the Holy Spirit for spiritual guidance rather than anything else. If Jesus is not God, then He is not lord over these other spiritual forces, but because He is, He can protect us from them and guide us through prayer and His word. Notice also in the Ephesians 1 passage, that the same power that the Father used to raise Jesus from the dead, is available for His people, the church to walk God's path (cf. Romans 8:11). This means in Christ, that we have been raised from spiritual death, that we have power to walk in newness of life, and that we will overcome death by God's power to also raise us to eternal life. We have power in the midst of our weakness to control our tongue, our temper, malice, greed, lust, jealousy or pride.[23] These attributes are often heightened in those who seek other spiritual 'power' or 'guidance'. But Jesus enables us to become better people, more like Him.

There is a connection, too, between knowledge of Christ and faith in Christ. *'Faith cannot grow without a firm basis of knowledge; knowledge is sterile if it does not bring forth faith.'*[24] The only knowledge and faith we need for spiritual truth are in Jesus. This power is also associated with the immeasurable love of Christ that surpasses knowledge, that we can know in our inner being through faith and be rooted to live in and show His love in our lives (3:16-20).

We then have power over evil in Christ's reign. This, at least, is freedom from evil spirituality and teachings. It may also imply the

---

[23] John Stott, *The Message of Ephesians*, The Bible Speaks Today (IVP: Leicester, 1973), p. 68.

[24] Stott, *The Message of Ephesians*, p. 67.

power to perform miracles given to some people. This is not something we can muster up ourselves; only if God sees fit to work through us in such ways. It is never to our glory but to God's glory. Any demonstration of miracles must be accompanied by true honouring of the lordship and glory of Jesus. That is how we can discern if they are truly from God. We should be aware that miracles can be false signs to lure people from the truth (2 Thessalonians 2:9-12). We must test such things against God's word and witness about Jesus.

Fourthly, Jesus is 'our Lord'. It is of utmost importance, therefore, that we acknowledge Him as both 'our Lord' and 'our Saviour', so we may rejoice in His coming, rather than be alarmed, ashamed and terrified when we have to stand before Him. Now is the day of salvation (2 Corinthians 6:2). What does this actually mean? Because Jesus is Lord over all things, including the church and even death, He is Lord of our eternal destiny; only He can save us and bring us into eternal life. We cannot simply wait until the Day of Judgement, we need our sins forgiven and to be willing to be part of His kingdom now, to have our names written in the Book of Life (Revelation 21:27). Otherwise, we will face eternal condemnation and separation from God (Revelation 20:11-15) by our own choice. It is not simply a matter of believing in God or that Christianity is true; it is about knowing God (John 17:3), wanting to be part of His coming kingdom, and letting Jesus be the Lord of our lives rather than following our own path, which always goes away from God and does not make us like Him. Other religions and philosophies may have good things to say about Jesus, but none of them recognise His status as Saviour and Lord.

There is also a more pastoral note here, which we have alluded to already, that we can trust Jesus has everything under His control when life seems out of control. This does not mean that Jesus controls and directs everything for its own sake, but that He directs history and our lives so that people may seek Him (Acts 17:26-27). Since nothing is outside His oversight, we can therefore bring our prayers and petitions to Jesus and to the Father. What is Jesus doing at God's right hand? Romans 8:34 tells us that Jesus is at the Father's side always interceding for those who are His. The Holy Spirit also intercedes for us by assisting us in our prayers (Romans 8:26-27). It is because of the grace of God given to us in Jesus, and because He shared in our sufferings, that we can confidently trust in Him to help us, to grant us mercy and grace in our time of need (Hebrews 4:14-16). What a marvellous thing that we are welcomed to approach the very throne of God and now have free access to do so in our Lord Jesus Christ, to be said to be seated with Him at the Father's right hand!

b) Jesus is to be worshipped

Several times after I became a Christian and started to attend church again, I experienced the love and presence of Jesus in very tangible ways. There were several occasions in worship in the church gathering where this happened, a real sense of the beauty of God and His love for me, which was emotional and profoundly uplifting. This is distinctly different from my previous time at church when I was younger, before I knew God.

There was also another occasion at home during a time of reading and devotion when I became overwhelmed by the presence of God in a mighty way. I was overawed at His greatness and was praising Him. I couldn't stand up and felt forced to bow. I ended up having to lie down for being somewhat physically faint, but I was overwhelmed by the Spirit and joy of the Lord and His great majesty. My muscles in my hands and wrists became immobile, my whole body felt like it was ecstatic, for lack of a better word, and it took over an hour before I was able to relax. I remember touching my forehead and hair, but it didn't feel normal; it felt like I was bathed in the pure radiance and light of God. At the same time, I sensed it was only the tip of the iceberg of His glory. No words can properly describe this experience, but I know it was from God, and it came at a time when I needed His comforting assurance.

When it comes to worshipping God, one question that some people ask is whether Jesus should be worshipped alongside God the Father. There is no denying that Jesus has been worshipped as God in the church for centuries, but some suggest there was a development of the worship of Jesus among early Christians, which did not become outright worship alongside God the Father until after the first disciples of Jesus.[25] The main problem with this is that if the first disciples of Jesus did not outright give Jesus worship alongside the Father, then the church could be seen as guilty of idolatry ever since. Yet, there is strong evidence to suggest Jesus does indeed deserve our worship and was indeed worshipped among the earliest Christians.

What we considered regarding the identity of Jesus as equal to God the Father directly, in the New Testament[26] and through the transference of Old Testament language about God to Jesus, and that Jesus is now seated on God's throne at the Father's right hand – all these give compelling evidence that Jesus was worshipped by these New Testament writers. This then becomes a precedent for the church subsequently. It is not worship of 3 gods, but the 3-in-1 Triune God.

It is worth pointing out that during His ministry, Jesus' identity was not evident to most. Peter and the other disciples

---

[25] James D. G. Dunn, *Did The First Christians Worship Jesus?*, (Louisville, SPCK, 2010), p. 90.

[26] Such as Philippians 2:9-11 and 1 Corinthians 8:6 which are considered some of the earliest New Testament writings.

See Larry W. Hurtado, *One God, One Lord: Early Christian Devotion and Ancient Jewish Monotheism*, (London: SCM, 1988), p.50 & 97.

struggled to understand the full extent of who Jesus was and what that meant. Even when Peter declared Jesus was the Messiah, He didn't understand that this meant Jesus had to die (Matthew 16:15-23). Jesus looked like a regular Jewish man. It was only in His miracles and His transfiguration that the disciples got a glimpse of His true nature. After Jesus calmed the storm, the disciples worshipped Him as the Son of God (Matthew 14:33), but it was only after Jesus was raised from the dead and appeared to His disciples that they fully understood who He was as Lord and Saviour (Luke 24:44-47). The disciples worshipped Jesus when He returned to heaven (Luke 24:52). What this tells us is that the disciples' experience of Jesus led them to understand who Jesus is and honour Him as God. It subsequently would have taken time for the earliest Christians to develop the language and theology to express what they had seen and were utterly convinced of; the later epistles begin to demonstrate their understanding (cf. 1 John 1:1-4). The fact that many of them were willing to die for their faith, declaring Jesus as Lord rather than worshipping Caesar as Lord, shows the conviction they had about the divinity of Jesus.

Including such profession of faith in Christ, Larry Hurtado also gives further evidence of the worship of Jesus by the first Christians in their acts and religious practices.[27] This, in particular, includes hymns and prayers to, or about, Jesus. Philippians 2:6-11 and Colossians 1:15-20 are such passages which are commonly seen as recounting early Christian hymns about Jesus, exalting Him above all others. The most striking and direct worship of Jesus is found in Revelation, such as 5:12-13,

> *"Worthy is the Lamb, who was slain, to receive power and wealth and wisdom and strength and honour and glory and*

---

[27] Hurtado, *TITLE* p. 99-100.

praise!' ... *'To him who sits on the throne and to the Lamb be praise and honour and glory and power, for ever and ever!"*

Most Christians today have not had the experiences of those first disciples, seeing the risen Jesus face to face, but we can rely on their testimony. It is a challenge to us: Do we have that same level of conviction about the deity of Jesus, based on the authority of their testimony passed down to us in the New Testament? Do we acknowledge who Jesus is in word and deed? Do we give Him the honour and glory He deserves for who He is and what He has done in saving us?

It is not just Christians who are called to worship Jesus. As Philippians 2:9-11 declares, all will bow to Him one day. There is a clear command to angels to worship Jesus in Hebrews 1:6 because He is greater than them, *"And again, when God brings his firstborn into the world, he says, 'Let all God's angels worship him."* Because Jesus is Lord, He is to be honoured and worshipped by all, since it is through Him that we all live (2 Corinthians 8:6). Some groups claim to be Christian, such as the Mormons and Jehovah's Witnesses, yet they do not acknowledge the Lordship of Jesus in worship. They need to reconsider the evidence and their position. Neither are other faiths valid because they all deny the reality of the deity of Jesus and His saving work for us, thus they cannot also worship the true God. If Jesus is Lord, no other can stand against Him. Even though other faiths may contain some truth, at the core they deny who Jesus is and what He has done, and so deny the revelation of God in Jesus as Lord and Saviour. All will one day recognise Him, whether gladly or in fear and regret.

c) Jesus is to be proclaimed

Another very significant consequence of Jesus' Lordship is that He must be proclaimed by His church as Saviour and Lord. Much can be said about the importance of evangelism, - heralding the Good News the Greek *'evangelizó'*.[28] Let us just note a few aspects briefly here.

The proclamation of the good news about Jesus, His salvation and Lordship, is not just something to be done by pastors and preachers in a church setting. No! As members of the body of Christ, all disciples are commissioned by the authority of Jesus with the task to proclaim the gospel and make more disciples, as the great universal task of His kingdom here on earth.

> *"Then Jesus came to them and said, 'All authority in heaven and on earth has been given to me. Therefore go and make disciples of all nations, baptising them in the name of the Father and of the Son and of the Holy Spirit, and teaching them to obey everything I have commanded you." (Matthew 28:18-20)*

If we do not engage in witnessing to people about Jesus, we are disobeying the command of Jesus. As John Wesley said, *'I look upon all the world as my parish; thus far I mean, that, in whatever part of it I am, I judge it meet, right, and my bounden duty to declare unto all that are willing to hear, the glad tidings of salvation.'* [29]

If God's people do not preach the good news about Jesus, then how will those who have not heard have a chance to respond, believe and be saved? As Romans 10:13-15 says,

> *"Everyone who calls on the name of the Lord will be saved. How, then, can they call on the one they have not believed in? And how can they believe in the one of whom they have not heard? And how can they hear without someone preaching to them? And how can anyone preach unless they are sent? As it is written: 'How beautiful are the feet of those who bring good news!"*

---

[28] https://biblehub.com/greek/2097.htm
[29] John Wesley, *Journal* (ed. N. Curnock), 11th June, 1739.

Some may say God will save all He wants to, or even all who are predestined. Jesus did say, *"No one can come to me unless the Father who sent me draws them"*, but God has commissioned us to make Jesus known. We cannot negate our responsibility and expect God to reveal Himself to all He chooses. There is a mysterious balance between God's supreme will, authority and action, and our human responsibility. God has graciously invited us to partake in His mission for the world. He did not need to, but He chose to, so let us see it as the privilege it is. Not all are evangelists in that sense, but all of us have the opportunity to testify about our faith and should be ready to testify to the reason for the hope that we have (1 Peter 3:15).

As the church more broadly, then, Jesus must always be the centre of both our worship and our preaching and teaching. If the church preaches a different Jesus or a different gospel than what has been passed down to us in the Bible, then we are frauds and are an offence to God (Galatians 1:6-9).

This is the missional dimension of the importance of Jesus' divine authority and eternal Lordship.

d) Jesus is to be followed

Our obedience to Jesus is not limited to testifying about Him. It stems from discipleship, meaning we follow Him and learn from Him. Many times, in the Gospels Jesus calls people to follow Him (e.g. Matthew 9:9; Mark 8:34; John 10:27). As God the Son, Jesus has divine authority in what He says, and complete understanding of human nature and life, meaning His word is relevant and gives wisdom to people of all ages and cultures. Obedience is a rather negative and forceful-sounding word. It is better to think of it as a matter of relationship and transformation of our inner being, our attitudes and the way we live, not simply observance of archaic rules. Consider the following passages:

"Come to me, all you who are weary and burdened, and I will give you rest. Take my yoke upon you and learn from me, for I am gentle and humble in heart, and you will find rest for your souls. For my yoke is easy and my burden is light." (Matthew 11:28-30)

"As the Father has loved me, so have I loved you. Now remain in my love. If you keep my commands, you will remain in my love, just as I have kept my Father's commands and remain in his love. I have told you this so that my joy may be in you and that your joy may be complete. My command is this: love each other as I have loved you." (John 15:9-12)

In the Matthew passage, Jesus calls us to come to Him, being weary and burdened, so we may find true rest. Whether it be from trying to strive to look good and meet people's expectations, trying to get to the top of the ladder, trying to please God, or whatever we do that makes us burdened. We see the gentle character of Jesus, one whom we can learn from to live well in God's world. His yoke is not oppressive like that of a vicious dictator, but easy and light. That does not mean it isn't personally challenging to follow Jesus' words and commands, but they do lead to life and flourishing.

As John states, to follow Jesus' commands is about remaining in His love and can be summed up as loving one another, just as Jesus has loved us. God's love is the fundamental and transformative principle that guides us in life to walk in God's ways. Doing so will make our joy complete and bring true freedom.

"To the Jews who had believed him, Jesus said, 'If you hold to my teaching, you are really my disciples. Then you will know the truth, and the truth will set you free." (John 8:31-32)

So, we have seen a fair few implications of the Lordship of Jesus in this chapter. He is above all others, we can trust Him to provide and care for us, and our response is to be of true worship and obedience to Jesus, as we grow in His love and live out His ways so others may also find the rest and freedom of being under the goodness of Jesus' reign.

Chapter 6. Jesus and the 'I am' sayings

In chapter 1, we referred to the connection of John's 'I am' sayings (Greek: *ego eimi*) to the Old Testament understanding of God. These are not just simple statements of identity, the phrase identifies the deity of Jesus and His eternal Lordship as *'The LORD'*, the eternal and creator God. The clearest of these statements is in John 8:58, where Jesus declares, "...*before Abraham was born, I am!*" This denotes the pre-existence of Jesus; it is made even clearer in that those listening to Jesus picked up stones to stone Him because they thought He was blaspheming in using the Name for God declared to Moses (Exodus 3:14 "I am who I am"); John 8:59, see also 5:18).

There are other occasions when Jesus uses the phrase which could be a simple statement of identity 'I am He' or 'It is Me', such as when Jesus calls to His fearful disciples when He came to them on the water (6:20) and when the Roman soldiers came to arrest Him (18:4-6).[30] Both of these incidents are in the context of displaying divine power, the second of which the soldiers fell to the ground after Jesus said, "I am He". Yet, it is the seven 'I am' sayings that are followed by a noun that truly stand out and give us insight into the significance of Jesus as God. These statements are either associated with a miracle/ sign, or are summary statements about Jesus, that *'the essence of all the signs is to reveal that Jesus is the true life of and for humanity, the revealer of that life, and the way to obtain that true (eternal) life.*[31] There are overlapping and repeated ideas in several of these statements, namely the theme of 'life'.

---

[30] Ben Witherington, *John's Wisdom: A Commentary on The Fourth Gospel*, (Louisville, KY, Westminster John Knox Press, 1995), p. 156-57.

[31] Witherington, *John's Wisdom*, p. 157.

a) I am the Bread of Life

"I am the bread of life. Whoever comes to me will never go hungry, and whoever believes in me will never be thirsty...I am the living bread that came down from heaven. Whoever eats this bread will live for ever. This bread is my flesh, which I will give for the life of the world." (John 6:35, 51)

This is part of a dialogue Jesus had with some of the Jews after the miracle of the 'Feeding the 5,000' (6:1-12). They followed Jesus because they were satisfied after eating the loaves and the fish (6:26). Some wanted to make Him king of Israel by force, but this was not His intention (6:13-14). Jesus told them, *"Do not work for food that spoils, but for food that endures to eternal life, which the Son of Man will give you..."* (6:27). The people had not believed, despite the sign He just performed. They wanted another sign like the miraculous provision of food God gave Israel in the wilderness (6:30-33)!

It is following this that Jesus declares He is *'the bread of life'*. He was not talking about physical bread, but a spiritual nourishment and satisfaction, that which the 'Feeding of the 5,000' was a physical illustration. This spiritual food *'endures to eternal life'*, unlike the miraculous provision of physical food, which only satisfies physical need for the day, which the people wanted. This spiritual nourishment is found only in Jesus. One must 'feed' on Jesus, believing in His saving work on the cross where He gave His body and shed His blood for us. Just as bread does us no good unless we eat it, so neither will the saving work of Christ unless we take it into our inner being for ourselves.

It is only because Jesus is God that He can give us the divine life which is in Him. *"In him was life, and that life was the light of all people" (1:4).* The Greek word *'zōē'* has this sense of eternal and divine life throughout the New Testament, and especially in John. It is far more than just biological life which we need, we also need spiritual and eternal life. Only Jesus is able to provide this for us. We each must appropriate this reality by taking Jesus into our hearts and believing in Him (6;40, 47).

b) I am the Light of the World

'I am the light of the world. Whoever follows me will never walk in darkness, but will have the light of life.' (John 8:12)

John likes to use contrasting terms often in his Gospel and First Letter. He speaks of *'light'* in his Gospel more than any other New Testament book. This contrast is meant to designate what is good and what is not good for us. The idea of light as something good is common to most people. That Jesus is the light of the whole world suggests He is more than just someone good or pleasant to listen to or learn from; He is the only source of true light (1:9) for all people. God Himself is light; there is no darkness in Him at all (1 John 1:5).

Light can be associated with creation, light being the first thing God made. It can also refer to knowledge about God or knowledge and wisdom from God to show us the way in a dark world (Psalm 119:105).[32] We noted above in John 1:4 that in Jesus is life, *"...that life is the light of all people."* The connection to giving spiritual and eternal life is a significant aspect of the light, the goodness that Jesus brings to the world. Just as light is needed for life to exist, so we need Jesus to have spiritual and eternal life.

The term also has in mind the idea of truth and moral goodness as we see in John 3:19-21,

"This is the verdict: light has come into the world, but people loved darkness instead of light because their deeds were

---

[32] Witherington, *John's Wisdom,* p. 174, 75.

evil. Everyone who does evil hates the light, and will not come into the light for fear that their deeds will be exposed. But whoever lives by the truth comes into the light, so that it may be seen plainly that what they have done has been done in the sight of God."

In Jesus is all truth and moral uprightness; there is no falsehood or sin in Him at all. This is why we can rely completely on Him, and everything written for us in God's word. It will never lead us astray, but we must beware of those who twist God's word and can lead us astray. John tells us in his first letter:

"This is the message we have heard from him and declare to you: God is light; in him there is no darkness at all. If we claim to have fellowship with him and yet walk in the darkness, we lie and do not live out the truth. But if we walk in the light, as he is in the light, we have fellowship with one another, and the blood of Jesus, his Son, purifies us from all sin." (1 John 1:5-7)

If we truthfully seek to follow Jesus, we will not walk in darkness and will have complete forgiveness of our sins. When we do walk in His light, we will have fellowship with God, which is indeed light and goodness; we receive the blessing of His life and light into our lives, which will guide us in life when we take hold of His word into our hearts. This also means that when life is tough, and things seem dark, troublesome or uncertain, we can trust in Jesus, knowing He will see us through because *"...the light shines in the darkness, and the darkness has not overcome it"* (John 1:5). His word will guide us. If not, even death could get rid of Jesus, then we can be assured that if we follow Him, we will have the light of life.

c) I am the Gate

"I am the gate for the sheep. All who have come before me are thieves and robbers, but the sheep have not listened to them. I am

the gate; whoever enters through me will be saved. They will come in and go out, and find pasture. The thief comes only to steal and kill and destroy; I have come that they may have life, and have it to the full." (John 10:7-10)

Before Jesus gets to the famous phrase that He is *'the good shepherd'*, He also declared that He is the gate by which people can enter into the kingdom of God, keeping with the shepherding metaphor. All other attempts to get into the kingdom of God are advocated by frauds and thieves, which Jesus was saying were the Pharisees at that time (also see Matthew 23:13). As the gate, Jesus also guards and protects those who are His, keeping them from being taken from Him. He protects His people from those who would seek to deceive and destroy them (10:28). No matter how many have tried, no one has been able to destroy the church, because it belongs to God. Nothing will be able to separate us from the love of God that is in Christ Jesus our Lord (Romans 8:37-39)!

d) I am the Good Shepherd

"I am the good shepherd. The good shepherd lays down his life for the sheep... I am the good shepherd; I know my sheep and my sheep know me..." (John 10:11, 14)

The understanding of shepherds is sometimes misconstrued in Western culture as being rather sentimental and soft, but the picture of shepherds in 1st century Palestine was a tiring, hard and sometimes dangerous job. The adjective 'good' here also likely depicts nobility and worthiness rather than soft and gentle.[33] A shepherd would protect and care for the sheep and lead them to places to pasture. Indeed, the noble and worthy shepherd would be willing to risk his life for the sheep by fending off a dangerous animal.

---

[33] D.A. Carson, *The Gospel According to John*, (Leicester, IVP, 1991), p. 386.

As the Shepherd of His people, Jesus cares for, provides for, and leads His people into good pasture, a place of rest and flourishing into the fullness of life. We can strive all we want to find true happiness and satisfaction in the things of the world, but they do not last and cannot truly fulfil our deepest needs.

As a teenager, I sought purpose and fulfilment, but nothing filled the void I felt until I met Jesus. He provided spiritual nourishment for me by His word and His life in me. We do not need to wander away to other spiritual teachings; they have no hope of fullness of life and will eventually lead us astray.

We have already mentioned that spiritual and eternal life is only available in Jesus, because He is God, and because, as both man and God, He laid down His life for His sheep. There could be no better Shepherd! The language of sheep here suggests we are in mortal danger (from judgement, death) and cannot save ourselves. We are also prone to wander astray if left to our own devices, following paths that do not lead to true life. We must get to know Jesus, to know His voice, His word, so we can recognise His way, and those who are bad shepherds who seek to destroy the sheep (10:5, 10).

The very language Jesus uses as being the Shepherd of God's people has strong resonance with Psalm 23 and Ezekiel 34. Here it is the LORD, the God of Israel, who is the Shepherd of His people (In Ezekiel in bringing Israel back from exile). Jesus is building on such passages as a framework for what He says here in John 10. He is claiming the same title as the LORD, as the Shepherd of God's people (Psalm 23:1). Because other leaders have proven to be bad shepherds (Ezekiel 34:1-10), God Himself promised He will shepherd His people (Ezekiel 34;11-12), a 'True Shepherd' was needed. He leads us into green and rich pastures (Psalm 23:2; Ezekiel 34:14-15). He guides us on the right paths

(Psalm 23:3). He brings back those who are lost, strengthens the weak and shepherds His flock with justice (Ezekiel 34:15-16). He gives security in the face of death (Psalm 23:4) because He Himself laid down His life to save us. He is our Shepherd and the sacrificial Lamb of God (John 1:29; Isaiah 40:11; Revelation 7:15-17). He gives us joy and blessing in Him, even though others will hate us (Psalm 23:5). And it is no longer just Israel He will shepherd, but people from all nations (John 10:16). One should reflect on these passages to fully appreciate what Jesus is saying.

e) I am the Resurrection and the Life

> *"I am the resurrection and the life. The one who believes in me will live, even though they die; and whoever lives by believing in me will never die." (John 11:25-26)*

Here, Jesus is speaking to Martha, the sister of Lazarus, who has just died. Jesus told Martha her brother would rise again, and Martha says she knows this will happen at the last day when God judges all people (11:23-24). This was taught by the prophets (e.g. Daniel 12:2). Now Jesus declares He Himself is the resurrection and the life. We have already seen that Jesus has the divine life in Himself as God, the '*zōē*' life. It makes sense then that in Jesus is the power to raise the dead. He showed this by raising Lazarus from the dead (11:43-44).

There is also a greater reality that Jesus speaks of here. The Father would raise Jesus from the dead, but as a man who would now longer die again, unlike Lazarus. Jesus is the first to raise from the dead and overcome death completely (Colossians 1:18; Revelation 1:18). As such, all who believe in Him will also be raised to everlasting life, even though we die physically. There is a physical resurrection. The Bible emphasises the reality of the physical resurrection, where we will receive new bodies, spiritual bodies (1 Corinthians 15:35-55). The two are not contradictory, spiritual in the Bible denotes of the Holy Spirit, or the new life that is in Christ, which is eternal and imperishable, unlike the fragile and transient nature of fallen life presently. And in Jesus we will 'never die' spiritually having been joined to the divine life of Jesus.

John 3:3 denotes this spiritual life, that when we believe in Jesus, we are *'born again'*, and thus no longer remain in spiritual death and exclusion from God. Ephesians 2:1-5 says,

"You were dead in your transgressions and sins... But because of his great love for us, God, who is rich in mercy, made us alive with Christ even when we were dead in transgressions – it is by grace you have been saved."

We are dead to God and separated from Him by sin in our natural state. In that state, we cannot make ourselves 'spiritually alive'. Only by His grace can we be reconciled to God and receive the life that is truly life.

f) I am the Way, the Truth, and the Life

"I am the way and the truth and the life. No one comes to the Father except through me." (John 14:6)

Jesus is here speaking to His disciples, that He is going to prepare a place for them in His Father's house (14:1-4). The disciples did not understand or know where Jesus was going, so He spelt it out plainly; He, Himself, is *"...the way and the truth and the life."* Once again, we see the emphasis on *'life'* which permeates John's gospel.

Jesus also declares He is *'the way'* to the Father, the only way. The early Christians were sometimes known as followers of 'the Way' (Acts 9:2). Because Jesus is God, it means there is no other way to God except through Him. God came to us in Jesus to reconcile us to Himself; only He can break the barrier of sin that keeps us from God; only He can destroy the power of death over us by His divine resurrection power.

This means all other religions, faiths and philosophies are not able to save us, because they do not acknowledge the reality of Jesus as Lord and Saviour. They may contain some elements of truth, but do not acknowledge this key truth about Jesus upon which everything about God and salvation stands. Jesus is the only one who can mediate between humans and God, being fully both.

In a similar note, Jesus is also *'the truth'*, not just *'a truth'*. In Him alone is all truth about God, about human existence, and about the way to God; nothing else is needed. Jesus also said, *"If you hold to my teaching, you are really my disciples. Then you will know the truth, and the truth will set you free" (John 8:31-32).* In Jesus and His teaching, we find all that we need and are called to be faithful in holding to His teaching above all. It does not need supplementing with other *'spiritual teaching'*. In Him we know the truth about God, about ourselves, about God's saving grace for us, and about eternal life. The truth of the gospel sets us free from not knowing these things, from the uncertainty of our standing before God, and brings us into the freedom of knowing God and being His beloved child.

g) I am the True Vine

> *"I am the true vine, and my Father is the gardener. He cuts off every branch in me that bears no fruit, while every branch that does bear fruit he prunes so that it will be even more fruitful... I am the vine; you are the branches. If you remain in me and I in you, you will bear much fruit; apart from me you can do nothing... As the Father has loved me, so have I loved you. Now remain in my love. If you keep my commands, you will remain in my love, just as I have kept my Father's commands and remain in his love." (John 15:1-2, 5, 9-10)*

This final *'I am'* saying uses a horticultural metaphor of a vine. A gardener will prune a vine, cutting off unfruitful branches, and pruning the rest of the vine so it can be more fruitful. Only branches connected to the vine can bear fruit. If a branch is cut off, it will wither and die because it has no nourishment from the sap coming from the roots through the trunk of the tree.

In the same way, Jesus says, we must bear fruit and remain in Him, otherwise we will be cut off and wither away. As Matthew 3:8 says, *"Produce fruit in keeping with repentance."* It is not those who claim to be Christians that belong to Jesus, but those who show it by a changed life. And in Matthew 7:17-19, we read,

"Every good tree bears good fruit, but a bad tree bears bad fruit. A good tree cannot bear bad fruit, and a bad tree cannot bear good fruit. Every tree that does not bear good fruit is cut down and thrown into the fire."

Jesus says you can recognise true disciples by whether their life and doctrine match. True and genuine faith will naturally produce positive changes, a desire to witness of Jesus, and good deeds in a person's life, which Paul describes as the fruit of the Spirit (Galatians 5:19-24). Such people the Father prunes, which may have in mind the idea of discipleship as well as the hardship we go through, so that we can be even more fruitful for God's kingdom. If we do not remain 'in Christ', we cannot bear spiritual fruit. We need to spend time with Him in prayer, in His word and in fellowship with other Christians to nourish our spiritual life.

The metaphor here extends primarily to the church as a whole. Jesus is speaking to the disciples in the second-person plural, not just individuals. This communal aspect of being disciples is sometimes lost or overshadowed in our modern Western society. It is important to remember we are called to be a community of disciples, learning and following the teachings of Jesus. If we do not partake in the community of disciples, we will be less fruitful for God's kingdom. Further, if churches do not remain in Jesus, in prayer and in His word, they will be cut off and lose their spiritual vigour and effectiveness. This is because we must remain connected to the source of our spiritual life in Jesus, both as individuals and church communities, otherwise churches will just dwindle away and die. The idea of 'remaining', or 'abiding' is frequent in John, making our home in Him and God with us. The requirement for doing so is shown here as faithfulness to Jesus' commands as evidence of abiding in His love.

There is perhaps also a secondary level, as with the 'bread of life', that has eucharistic overtones,[34] a symbolic reference in the Lord's Supper. Taking the Lord's Supper should not be seen as the primary focus of these sayings, as the qualification of being in the 'Vine' is primarily one of love and faith, as the context demands.[35]

To summarise then, in Jesus we receive His divine life, which connects us to God, to know Him, having spiritual nourishment and life to the full. We have the light of life, the full truth about God and salvation in Jesus alone. He is the only way to God and eternal life with God. Jesus tends and cares for us and assures us nothing can separate us from His love if we remain in Him, individually and as the church. We must remain close to Him through prayer, reading the Bible, and Christian fellowship.

---

[34] Raymond E. Brown, *The Gospel According to John I-XII*, (Geoffrey Chapman, London, 1975), p. 672-74 and Vol 2 John XIII-XXI, The Gospel according to John, (New Haven, NJ: Yale University Press, 1970/2008) pp. 675-677.
[35] Brown, *The Gospel*, p. 673-74.

Chapter 7. Jesus is 'God with us'

We have seen how in Jesus, God becomes 'God with us' in all we are (Heb. 4:16). God suffered for us in Jesus and is able to therefore identify with us in our suffering. He can bring us much comfort and encouragement as His people, to know the joy of the Lord is our strength (Nehemiah 8:10), who will never leave or forsake His people (John 14:18; Hebrews 13:5). Knowing the presence of God in our daily life is the reality of the Christian. Even when it is not apparent Jesus is with us, we can trust in His promise that He will see us through whatever we face. It is not based on feeling but on God's promise.

I have experienced myself on a couple of occasions in particular the reality of God's promise to be with me and strengthen me in a time of hardship. On one of these occasions there were a lot of troubling circumstances going on around me. I felt very troubled and weighed down. One night I came across a verse in Isaiah, *"Do not fear, for I am with you; do not be dismayed, for I am your God. I will strengthen you and help you; I will uphold you with my righteous right hand"* (41:10). It was extremely helpful for me at just the right time. I had a real sense of God's peace, that He is utterly dependable, that He will indeed be with me and strengthen me, which He did.

The reality of knowing God is with us is a reality rooted in God's promises and purpose for human life ever since He created the world and fulfilled in Jesus Christ, who is God become human to be with us in the present and the future hope of eternity with Him in glory. From Creation to this New Creation, stretches the biblical theme of 'God with us.

a) God's desire to be with us

In the beginning when God created the world and all of life, He made human beings stewards of the earth.

"So God created human beings in his own image, in the image of God he created them; male and female he created them. God blessed them and said to them, 'Be fruitful and increase in number; fill the earth and subdue it. Rule over the fish in the sea and the birds in the sky and over every living creature that moves on the ground." (Genesis 1:27-28)

Notice here how human beings were and are made in God's image, bearing the likeness of God the Creator and Father of us all. He even formed the man out of the dust of the earth and breathed His own life into Him (2:7). Humans were given authority to rule over the earth. Not to rule however we want, but in partnership with God in overseeing the earth, under the authority of His reign. There is then a closeness between God and humans in likeness, in relationship and in partnership to reign over the earth.

b) The dilemma of separation

However, when human beings sinned, this closeness was broken. Adam and Eve hid from God after eating from the Tree of the Knowledge of Good and Evil (3:7) and were subsequently banished from God's presence and access to the Tree of Eternal Life (3:22-24). The image of God in the creation account is linked with the authority to rule over the earth as God's representatives. This includes moral character, a desire for goodness in the world, wisdom to understand the world, and an eternal value of all humans, which demands we treat other humans with dignity and respect. Even though human beings are still considered to be in the image of God, which is the reason murder is forbidden (9:6), this image is presently marred by sin and death after humanity rebelled against God and broke their relationship with Him.

This is the great dilemma of human existence. This explains why God seems distant from us, so that we cannot see God or know what He is like except through the natural created order. Yet even this knowledge is distorted (Romans 1:19-21), even to the point that we can believe there is no God. The Bible, however, clearly shows us this is only because of sin and our desire to live our own way, hating the very idea of our accountability to God (Romans 1:21-23; 3:19; John 3:19-21). This dilemma is what the biblical story reveals to us, and that it was always God's intention to bring human beings back into a positive relationship with Him, back into His eternal presence. This is at least one way of describing the overarching story of the Bible, to which Jesus is the culmination.

c) God's plan to dwell with His people

After God banished human beings from His presence, He didn't remain distant and abstract; He instead set in motion a plan to reconcile us to Himself. As early as Genesis 5, we get a glimpse of someone who walked faithfully with God, enjoying His presence, so much so that He was one of only 2 people to never die, because God took Him from this world (5:21-24). This plan God enacted by first calling Abram, through whom God promised His blessing would go out to all nations (Genesis 12:1-3). He also promised to make Abram into a great nation, Israel, which would become a vehicle of God's blessing to the world (Exodus 19:4-6). In the covenant God made with Israel, He promised to be with them and be their God.

"I will walk among you and be your God, and you will be my people." (Leviticus 26:12)

This was seen most transiently in God dwelling among His people in the Tabernacle. Both in the completion of the Tabernacle and later the temple in Jerusalem, God's glory and presence came and filled the place where He promised to dwell with His people

(Exodus 40:34-35; 1 Kings 8:10-11). Even so, God's presence cannot be limited to one particular place, there is nowhere one can go where God doesn't see (Psalm 139:7-11). He is the God of the whole earth. People could walk closely with God and know something of His presence, but the temple was the focal point where God dwelt among His people. Yet, there was a greater reality of God's presence still to come.

Throughout Israel's history, the Israelites consistently failed to keep the covenant with God. God eventually departed from the temple (Ezekiel 10:18; 11:23), and Israel ended up in exile. Throughout all this long period, God had continued to warn Israel of the consequences of abandoning Him by sin, social injustice and idol worship. Yet at the same time, God continued to promise He would restore His people to the land and to walk faithfully with Him again (e.g. Jeremiah 31:31-34; Isaiah 40:1-11). But when Israel eventually returned from exile and the second temple was completed, God's glory did not fill it as had been the case previously (Ezra 3:10-13). As many of the later prophets made clear, there was still another act of God to come. God would come to His people, gathering them from all nations to see His glory (Isaiah 66:18), and His blessing of salvation would finally extend to the whole earth (Isaiah 49:6).

d) Jesus came to us as 'God with us'

It is into this prophetic expectation that Jesus enters. Isaiah had promised King Ahaz 730 years earlier than Jesus that God would give a sign of a Child being born to a mother miraculously to be called *'Immanuel (which means 'God with us')*. In fulfilment of Old Testament promises, Joseph was told to call Jesus Emmanuel, as well as 'Jesus' meaning Saviour (Matthew 1:23). In Jesus, God has now come to us, to save His people from their sins (1:21). The implications of this are for human beings to be restored into positive relationship with God and to enjoy His presence again through the saving work of Jesus Christ, which is for all who believe in Him. Matthew shows us this too at the end of his gospel, emphasising it as having significant importance for Jesus' coming. Jesus was with His disciples for 3 years during His ministry before His death, resurrection and ascension back into heaven. Before He returned to the Father, He said to His disciples,

> *"All authority in heaven and on earth has been given to me. Therefore go and make disciples of all nations, baptising them in the name of the Father and of the Son and of the Holy Spirit, and teaching them to obey everything I have commanded you. And surely I am with you always, to the very end of the age."*
> (Matthew 28:18-20)

Along with the command to disciple, baptise and teach people of all nations the words of Jesus and the good news about Him, is the promise that *'I am with you always'*. Yet, if Jesus has gone back into heaven, how is He still with us as His disciples today? This was not simply a promise for the disciples then, either. It is by His presence and indwelling of the person of the Holy Spirit. This is explained most clearly in John's gospel.

> *"If you love me, keep my commands. And I will ask the Father, and he will give you another advocate to help you and be with you forever— the Spirit of truth. The world cannot accept him, because it neither sees him nor knows him. But you know him, for he lives with you and will be in you."* (John 14:15-17)

The promise of Jesus to His disciples, not just those with Him during His ministry, is the promise of the Holy Spirit, by whom we will have God with us always. Notice again the connection with following the commands of Jesus, not as a way to earn God's presence, but that in loving Jesus and seeking to walk faithfully with Him, we will foster a greater closeness with Him, and know His presence more intimately in our daily life. To truly know this reality, one must experience God's Holy Spirit themselves, and the personal relationship with God we can now have in and through Jesus.

e) Salvation as 'God with us'

Even more, John gives us fascinating insight into Jesus in the opening of His gospel. He describes Jesus as *'the Word of God (John 1:1)'*. This use of 'the Word' relates Jesus to God's work of creation, revelation and salvation in the first 18 verses of John's gospel, which draws on Old Testament use of God's Word (e.g. Psalm 33:1-9; 107:20). The Word is the One who is now bringing about the new creation, who fully reveals God, and who establishes salvation for all people. John's gospel, *'presents Jesus as the incarnation of [the word of God] continuing [God's] work of revelation, healing, and creation'*.[36] The key interest for us here is found in John 1:14,

> *"The Word became flesh and made his dwelling among us. We have seen his glory, the glory of the one and only Son, who came from the Father, full of grace and truth."*

There are several key points here. Firstly, we see that John is talking about the incarnation of Jesus, His coming into the world in the virgin birth as a flesh and blood person. The Word who was with God and who is God, through whom all things exist (1:1-3), has now physically entered the world as a human, becoming flesh just as we are. This identification with humanity shows God's intent to save and reconcile us to Himself and be with us.

So, secondly, He made His dwelling among us. This may seem like a generic statement, but John is showing something remarkable here. The Greek word John uses is *'skénoō'*, which

---

[36] Alan. R. Culpepper, *Anatomy of the Fourth Gospel*, (Fortress Press, 1983), p. 106.

means to pitch one's tent.[37] This is the same root as the word used in the Greek translation of the Old Testament (LXX) for the Tabernacle, where God dwelt among the Israelites. John's usage of this verb, which occurs nowhere else in the New Testament outside of Revelation, highlights the theme of God's dwelling among His people and His desire and initiative to do so, just as He did with Israel.

Thirdly, John and his fellow disciples saw the glory of God in Jesus, which relates back to the glory of God filling the Tabernacle and the first temple. The reason this did not happen when the second temple was being completed may indeed be because God was waiting to reveal His glory afresh in the person of Jesus Christ. Jesus declared that His body was the new temple of God (John 2:21), the new hotspot of God's presence, because He is Himself God. Jesus is the one and only Son of God who reveals the Father's glory. This also has strong resonances with God revealing His glory to Moses on Mount Sinai (Exodus 33:18-23).

Fourthly, this glory is not just in physical appearance, it is in the revealing of the very nature and character of God. When God passed in front of Moses there was indeed a physical manifestation of God's glory, but what God said was, in fact, a declaration of His character, *"The LORD, the LORD, the compassionate and gracious God, slow to anger, abounding in love and faithfulness..."*(Exodus 34:6). The wording of *'abounding in love and faithfulness'* is very similar to John 1:14 that Jesus came *'full of grace and truth'*. John uses this resemblance to tell us God's covenant love and faithfulness are now revealed and seen fully in Jesus.[38] The emphasis of John's opening

---

[37] https://biblehub.com/greek/4637.htm
[38] See further: D. A. Carson, *The Gospel According to John*, (Leicester, IVP, 1991), p. 126-28.

verses '*is on the revelation of the Word [Jesus] as the ultimate disclosure of God himself.*'[39]

What the gospel writers are declaring then, helps us to see that Jesus as *'God with us'*, is not only that God was physically present on earth at some time in history, but His coming also fulfils God's ancient promises and initiative to bring us back into His presence, which we can know in a new and intimate relation with God by the Holy Spirit. Jesus reveals the truth about God and reveals what He is like, which is a key aspect of His glory. Jesus Himself has become the new dwelling place of God to whom we can now come, and through whom we can know God. He is the only Way, the fullness of all truth, and the Giver of all life (John 10:10; 14:6).

Not only so, but the New Testament also tells us that as God's people, we are now a temple of the Holy Spirit. This is true both of individual believers, *'Do you not know that your bodies are temples of the Holy Spirit, who is in you, whom you have received from God?'* (1 Corinthians 6:19), and of the church as the body of Christ, *'Don't you know that you yourselves are God's temple and that God's Spirit lives among you?'* (1 Corinthians 3:16). The Holy Spirit is a seal and a deposit from God, guaranteeing our future inheritance (2 Corinthians 1:22). It is important, therefore, that we walk in faithfulness and truth before God, otherwise, we can dampen the Spirit's presence in our life. As a church, there is still the possibility that Jesus may remove His presence altogether like God did from the Jewish temple (Revelation 2:5).

f) God's eternal dwelling with His people

There is one final part to the biblical story where we shall conclude. Just as God's presence was with humans in the beginning,

---

[39] Carson, *The Gospel*, p. 135.

and in the fulfilment of everything God has done in between, so the biblical story concludes with God's dwelling with His people forever in the New creation. We mentioned how the Greek word *'skēnoō'* is only used in John 1:14 outside of Revelation. In Revelation, it is used 4 times in reference to God's dwelling place. The final one of these is in Revelation 21:1-4,

> *"Then I saw 'a new heaven and a new earth,' for the first heaven and the first earth had passed away, and there was no longer any sea. I saw the Holy City, the new Jerusalem, coming down out of heaven from God, prepared as a bride beautifully dressed for her husband. And I heard a loud voice from the throne saying, 'Look! God's dwelling-place [noun: skēnē] is now among the people, and he will dwell [skēnoō] with them. They will be his people, and God himself will be with them and be their God. 'He will wipe every tear from their eyes. There will be no more death' or mourning or crying or pain, for the old order of things has passed away."*

This is a truly remarkable promise and hope for us to hold on to. That we can one day be in the fullness of God's presence, to dwell with Him in eternity on the renewed earth. This is what all our deepest hopes and desires as human beings point to, and where they will be completely filled! Heaven is not just a place; it is where our Lord Jesus is!

Conclusion

In summary, why then does it matter that Jesus is divine? The material we have examined is not exhaustive, but it has given us, I think, the key answers to our question.

As we saw to begin with, the deity of Jesus is occasionally explicit in the New Testament, but more often than not, the deity of Jesus is seen in the language used of Jesus and the acts He performs, both of which are used of the God of Israel in the Old Testament. God revealed Himself to Israel but has now revealed Himself to the world in Jesus Christ, who is the exact representation of God's Being. He has done this by coming to Earth as one of us and showing us who God is in His character and saving power for humanity.

This salvation is bringing people back into right relation with God through the death and resurrection of Jesus, enabling forgiveness, eternal life, and for people to know God personally.

In dying for us, Jesus suffered for us, showing He is not distant from the suffering of humanity but entered willingly into it. God cares about our suffering and has set a plan in place to one day do away with suffering, death and evil entirely. In the meantime, we can depend on God's grace and help to find mercy in our time of need, having the comfort and hope of God's kingdom when we depend on Him.

The deity of Jesus also means He is Lord over all, even spiritual forces and all human rulers; all are accountable to Him. For this reason, Jesus is worthy of worship. He's of central importance in the witness of the church, and in our lives to follow His teaching with a loving obedience for what He has done for us.

John's gospel in particular highlights some key realities of Jesus as God, the great I Am: the One who gives us divine life, life to the full, eternal life; the One who gives us the light of life and knowledge of the truth and of God; the One who cares for us as the Good Shepherd and willingly laid down His life for us; the One who is the only way to the Father, who Himself is life and truth; and the One who holds His people together and gives them life as the true Vine.

Most broadly, the entire biblical narrative points to the reality of God's desire to dwell with humanity. He dwelt among the Israelites in the Tabernacle and the Temple, but He came as one of us as 'the Word become flesh' that we may see and know God in Jesus. He has promised to be with us in the present by His Holy Spirit, and one day, we will dwell with God in His heavenly kingdom and new creation in perfection and glory. This is the Christian hope and the gospel of Jesus we are to share!

Bibliography

Bauckham, Richard, *Jesus and The God of Israel : God Crucified and Other Studies on The New Testament's Christology of Divine Identity*, (Milton Keynes, Paternoster, 2008).

Brown, Raymond. E., *The Gospel According to John I-XII*, (Geoffrey Chapman, London, 1975).

Brown, Raymond. E., *The Gospel According to John XIII-XXI*, (New Haven, NJ: Yale University Press, 1975/2008).

Carson, D. A., *The Gospel According to John*, (Leicester, IVP, 1991).

Culpepper, Alan. R., *Anatomy of the Fourth Gospel*, (Fortress Press, 1983).

Dunn, James D. G., *Did The First Christians Worship Jesus?*, (Louisville, SPCK, 2010).

Hurtado, Larry W., *One God, One Lord: Early Christian Devotion and Ancient Jewish Monotheism*, (London: SCM, 1988).

Jersak, Bradley, A *More Christlike God*, (Plain Truth Ministries, Pasadena, 2015).

Keck, Leander E., *Genesis, Exodus, Leviticus*, The New Interpreter's Bible, vol. 1, (Nashville, TN, Abingdon Press, 1994).

Köstenberger, Andreas J., Merkle, Benjamin L., and Plummer, Robert L., *Going Deeper with New Testament Greek*, (Nashville, B&H Academic, 2016).

Lincoln, Andrew, *The Gospel According to St. John*, (London, Hendrickson Publishers, 2005).

Mann, Alan, *Atonement for a Sinless Society*, (James Clark & Co. Cambridge, 2016).

Stott, John, *The Message of Ephesians*, The Bible Speaks Today: (IVP: Leicester, 1973).

Webb, Barry, *The Message of Zechariah*, The Bible Speaks Today: (IVP: Leicester, 2003).

Wesley, John, *Journal* (ed. N. Curnock), 11th June, 1739.

Witherington, Ben, *John's Wisdom: A Commentary on the Fourth Gospel*, (Louisville, KY: Westminster John Knox Press, 1995).

Wright, Christopher. J. H., *Knowing God Through The Old Testament*, (Downers Grove, IL: IVP, 2019).

Web sources:

https://biblehub.com/

https://billmuehlenberg.com/2023/06/23/tim-keller-on-suffering-and-evil/

Dr. C. Fred Smith, *The Suffering of Christ on the Cross in the Theology of Jürgen Moltmann*. https://urnottheonlyone.com/2017/07/11/the-suffering-of-christ-on-the-cross-in-the-theology-of-jurgen-moltmann/

John Lennox in '*Oxford Mathematician DESTROYS Atheism (15 Minute Brilliancy!)*' https://www.youtube.com/watch?v=VrIvwPConv0&list=WL&index=6

John Wesley, *Journal* (ed. N. Curnock), 11th June, 1739. https://www.ldolphin.org/silence.html

www.ingramcontent.com/pod-product-compliance
Lightning Source LLC
Chambersburg PA
CBHW061224070526
44584CB00029B/3970